Writing about

CW01084275

In this book, Graham Connah
ological authorship: its diversity, its challenges and its methodology. Based on his own experiences, he presents his personal
views about the task of writing about archaeology. The book
is not intended to be a technical manual. Instead, Connah aims
to encourage archaeologists who write about their subject to
think about the process of writing. He writes with the beginning
author in mind, but the book will be of interest to all archaeologists who plan to publish their work. Connah's overall premise
is that those who write about archaeology need to be less concerned with content and more concerned with how they present
it. It is not enough to be a good archaeologist. One must also
become a good writer and be able to communicate effectively.
Archaeology, he argues, is above all a literary discipline.

Graham Connah is a Visiting Fellow in the School of Archaeology and Anthropology at the Australian National University
in Canberra. A scholar of the archaeology of Africa and Australia, he is the author of eight books and founded the journal
Australasian Historical Archaeology.

Writing about Archaeology

GRAHAM CONNAH
Australian National University

CAMBRIDGE
UNIVERSITY PRESS

CAMBRIDGE UNIVERSITY PRESS
Cambridge, New York, Melbourne, Madrid, Cape Town, Singapore,
São Paulo, Delhi, Dubai, Tokyo

Cambridge University Press
32 Avenue of the Americas, New York, NY 10013-2473, USA

www.cambridge.org
Information on this title: www.cambridge.org/9780521688512

© Graham Connah 2010

This publication is in copyright. Subject to statutory exception
and to the provisions of relevant collective licensing agreements,
no reproduction of any part may take place without the written
permission of Cambridge University Press.

First published 2010

Printed in the United States of America

A catalog record for this publication is available from the British Library.

Library of Congress Cataloging in Publication Data

Connah, Graham.
Writing about archaeology / Graham Connah.
    p.   cm.
Includes bibliographical references and index.
ISBN 978-0-521-86850-1 (hbk.) – ISBN 978-0-521-68851-2 (pbk.)
1. Archaeology–Authorship.   2. Written communication.
3. Archaeological literature–Publishing.   I. Title.
CC82.C66   2010
930.1–dc22   2009022685

ISBN 978-0-521-86850-1 Hardback
ISBN 978-0-521-68851-2 Paperback

Cambridge University Press has no responsibility for the persistence or
accuracy of URLs for external or third-party Internet Web sites referred to in
this publication and does not guarantee that any content on such Web sites is,
or will remain, accurate or appropriate.

Dedicated to the memory of

George Burr Perrett
Fellow of Selwyn College, Cambridge,
from 1920 to 1964

'O! that mine enemy would write a book! has been a well known prayer against an enemy. I had written a book, and it has furnished matter for abuse for want of something better.'

Thomas Jefferson, third president of the United States, in a letter to Dr Samuel Brown, 25 March 1798 (Peden 1955: xxiv).

Contents

Figures   *page* ix

Preface and Acknowledgements   xi

One
Creating the canon
The integral role of writing in archaeology
1

Two
Learning from others
Archaeological writers past and present
11

Three
Readership determines form
For whom are we writing?
43

Four
Turning data into text
Images of the past
59

Five
The process of writing
10 percent inspiration, 90 percent perspiration
72

Six
Visual explanation
Pictures that should talk
91

Seven
Pleasing everyone
Writing for different types of publication
136

Eight
Publishers, editors and referees
Devils incarnate or guardian angels?
158

Nine
The publication process
Creating a quality product
172

Ten
The aftermath
Reviewers and readers
184

References   191

Index   205

Figures

1. Deserted medieval village.   *page* 106
2. Excavated Iron Age house.   107
3. Section through a ditch and rampart.   108
4. Excavated hurdle.   109
5. Excavation in progress.   110
6. Excavated burial of an adult and two children.   111
7. Potsherds with dotted wavy-line patterns.   112
8. Sailing ship and anchor on a smoking pipe.   113
9. Detail on a silver bowl.   113
10. Scanning electron micrograph of gold granules.   114
11. Wooden sculpture of a man's head.   115
12. Cormac's Chapel, Cashel, Co. Tipperary, Ireland.   116
13. Stone carving of an unknown saint.   117
14. Detail of a hammerbeam roof.   118
15. Remains of the Dutch East Indiaman *Amsterdam*.   119
16. Conservation in progress at Stonehenge in 1958.   120
17. Map by H. A. Shelley, drawn for *Antiquity*.   121
18. Map of mottes (medieval castle mounds).   122

19. Plan of Portchester Castle, Hampshire, England.   123
20. Plan of excavated village at Skara Brae, Orkney.   124
21. Isometric drawing of West Kennet Long Barrow.   126
22. Section drawing of Iron Age pit at Maiden Castle.   128
23. Selection of Australian stone artefacts.   129
24. Roman pots from Little Chester, Derbyshire.   130
25. Drawing of the back of a bronze mirror.   131
26. Rock painting showing Europeans and Bushmen.   132
27. Diagram of calibrated radiocarbon dates.   133
28. Occurrence through time of shipwrecks.   133
29. Recovered skeletal elements of aurochs.   134
30. Table showing seasonal availability of resources.   134
31. Table listing Mesolithic dwelling places.   135

Preface and Acknowledgements

I wrote this book in 2007 and 2008 following a suggestion in 2005 by Simon Whitmore, formerly an editor at Cambridge University Press. I am grateful to him and to Beatrice Rehl, the present Humanities and Social Sciences editor at Cambridge University Press, New York, for their advice and patience during its gestation. It has been a great pleasure to continue my long and fruitful association with the Press.

It seemed arrogant and patronizing to write a book telling other archaeologists how to write, and I have remained acutely aware of this throughout my work on it. However, in no way should this book be thought of as a manual of instructions. This is certainly not intended. Rather the book consists of my own reflections on the task after more than a half-century of attempting to write about archaeology. My intention has been to encourage archaeological authors to think more critically about what they do and how they do it. I suggest that in order to write well about archaeology it is not enough to be an archaeologist; one must also learn how to write and each of us might achieve this in our own way. This opinion has been shaped by my contact with many other members of the archaeological profession over the years, too many to acknowledge here but all owed a debt of gratitude; to an extent each one of us is the sum of those we have known. With this in mind the book is dedicated not to an archaeologist but to the memory of an historian, remembered for his insistence on rigour in writing.

I would like to thank no less than five anonymous publisher's 'readers' who commented on my proposal for the book and whose opinions influenced the way that it was subsequently written. I am also particularly grateful to David Pearson of the National Library of Australia, Canberra, and to Michael West-away of the Queensland Museum, Brisbane, who both commented on an earlier version of the book and whose suggestions have influenced its final form.

The illustrations included in Chapter 6 need some explanation. With such a limited number, it was clearly impossible to provide comprehensive examples of the great diversity of visual material used in archaeological publications. I spent many days making a selection that can only be representative in the most general way, but the images that I chose were all ones that caught my attention and *told* me something, as I think archaeological illustrations should.

The increasingly complex matter of copyright also limited the choice of illustrations, and it will be observed that they are drawn from only a few publications. In particular, it seemed inappropriate to use my own material, and in general I avoided doing so. The sources of the illustrations I have used are acknowledged in their captions, and I am grateful to all those individuals, publications and institutions that allowed me to reproduce their material. Particular thanks are due to the editors of *Antiquity*, *The Antiquaries Journal* and the *Proceedings of the Prehistoric Society*, from which the majority of the illustrations came. Specific acknowledgements are also due to Malcolm Thurlby, for permission to use his photograph reproduced in Figure 12, and to John Crook for permission to use his photograph reproduced in Figure 14. Although every effort has been made to obtain permission to reproduce copyright items, in some cases, because of the passage of time or other circumstances, this has not been possible. The author and publishers would be glad to hear from any copyright holders who have not been acknowledged. I would also like to thank Neal McCracken and Stuart Hay, photographers at the Australian National University, Canberra, for digital work on the illustrations, continuing the skilled assistance that they have given me for so many other publications. Similarly I am grateful to Douglas Elford, of the National Library of Australia, for technical assistance with Figure 8.

In addition, I wish to thank the School of Archaeology and Anthropology at the Australian National University, in Canberra, at which I have been a Visiting Fellow for some years. While writing this book I was also grateful for Kevin MacDonald's help, when he arranged my access to the library of the Institute of Archaeology at University College London.

Finally, I must once more thank Beryl Connah, my partner for almost five decades, for reading chapters, compiling the index and tolerating a husband who simply refuses to stop writing.

One

Creating the canon

The integral role of writing in archaeology

Writing about archaeology is the archaeologist's most lasting contribution to society. In less than two hundred years, archaeology has fundamentally changed most people's understanding of the human past and the way in which many of us view ourselves. It has made vital contributions to our consciousness of who we are and where we are. In the long term, however, this has been accomplished not merely by the excavations, field surveys and variety of analyses that are usually thought of as the core of archaeological endeavour but by the presentation of such work and its results in one or another published form. As Joyce et al. (2002: 6–7), citing Walter Taylor (1948: 34–35) and James Deetz (1988: 15–20), have pointed out, the very word 'archaeology' covers two different activities, in which 'the writing of archaeology [is] as integral to the production of archaeological knowledge as encounters in the field'. Indeed, the discipline of archaeology consists of the body of published material that has been built up by many thousands of writers, many of whom are now dead, creating a massive data base from which we can

1

retrieve information and which we constantly augment, correct and revise. This data base constitutes the archaeological 'canon', meaning neither a misspelled antiquated weapon nor a member of the Christian clergy but a generally recognized body of publications that are central to research and teaching in our discipline and that form a material expression of its scholarship.

Therefore it is the creation and continual expansion of this archaeological canon that should be the major objectives for practitioners of the discipline. For this reason, the necessity for archaeologists to publish their work has long been widely accepted. An early exponent of this view was the exemplary publicist Pitt Rivers (1898: 28), who famously stated, 'A discovery dates only from the time of the record of it, and not from the time of its being found in the soil'. More recently, White (1983: 171) trenchantly insisted, 'Research which is not available for others to use does not exist.... If you do not write it down it does not exist. The converse is also true: what you report and publish is all that exists'. Consequently, it is hardly surprising that publication has become an essential element in career building for professional archaeologists, particularly those working in the academic sector. As with other disciplines, the 'publish or perish' syndrome is widespread, sometimes resulting in more haste than care and the risk of an outcome that might be described as 'publish *and* perish'!

As an academic archaeologist with a long career in research and teaching, I have been writing about my subject for more than fifty years, although regrettably only in English – though sometimes translated by others, into Japanese (1993a), German (2006), and French (2008). My first published item was in 1954, at the age of nineteen, although the obscurity of the outlet has long protected me from subsequent embarrassment (Connah 1954). Since then I have been the author of research monographs (Connah 1975, 1981a, 1996a, 2007, 2009); and general syntheses (1987, 1988, 1993b, 2001a), an editor or collaborating author of specific site studies (1997, Connah, Rowland and Oppenheimer 1978) and the author of an introductory 'popular' text (2004a, 2006, 2008). In addition, I have written some hundreds of journal papers, notes, book reviews and other minor items, some of the journal papers in collaboration with other writers. Furthermore,

I have edited two monographs (1983, 1998), founded a journal that I edited for seven issues (1983–1988, 1996b), been an assistant editor of another journal for three issues (1971–1973) and refereed many papers for a variety of journals in a number of countries. This review of my own writing career is not mere egotism. Rather, it is provided as evidence that by now I should have learnt a little about archaeological writing, but in fact it has been a long and hard road, at times steep, rough and beset with accident black spots. Many contemporaries, including some more productive and more distinguished than me, would I suspect admit to a similar experience.

For most of us, these problems were particularly severe during the earliest part of our careers, and when talking to younger colleagues, engaged in postgraduate research or in their first posts, I constantly hear remarks about how difficult they find the writing process. As many editors would concede, there are also some archaeologists who are further advanced in their careers who nevertheless have similar problems, although they often refuse to admit them. As for the real beginners, such as undergraduates engaged in third- or fourth-year studies, there are even those who seem to think that 'the archaeology is fun [frankly, I have never found it so] if only one did not have to write about it as well'.

Yet, as already indicated, writing about archaeology is an inseparable and central part of the archaeologist's task. As Anthony Sinclair has put it, 'Archaeologists, like anthropologists, write; we create our subject' (Sinclair 1989: 161). To be able to do this successfully, it is not enough for us to understand the often highly complex archaeological data and be able to present, analyse and interpret it in an orderly manner; we must also learn how to write; specifically, we must learn how to write about archaeology. The immediate difficulty is that there are so many ways of doing this. Not only will individual approaches to the task often differ but the task itself will also vary depending on the character of the subject matter and on the purpose and intended readership of what is being written. Furthermore, the ways that archaeologists have written about their subject have changed over time and will continue to change. There are distinct genres of archaeological writing that constitute more than variations in literary style, reflecting as they do the cultural background and theoretical stance of the writers, as well as the character of the content.

However, the central problems of archaeological writing are also familiar to writers of history and probably to writers in other disciplines. As long ago as the sixteenth century Girolamo Cardano, natural philosopher, medical man and astrologer, as well as a practising historian, wrote,

> It is very hard to write history, and it is therefore rare. First of all, because of the need for skill and style and practice; second, because of that for diligence and effort in chasing down the smallest points; third, because of that for judgement. (Translated by Grafton 2007: 183 from the Latin original.)

Cardano's perceptive remarks would apply equally to modern archaeological writing as to historical writing. He correctly identified the conflicting requirements of such writing: the need to write well, the need to include all the relevant data (of which too much will bore the reader but too little will leave the reader in ignorance) and the need to analyse and interpret the data. It is the task of balancing these obligations that often makes writing about archaeology so problematic. The need to provide both detailed technical information or theoretical content, and extended discussion of alternative interpretations, can make it extremely difficult to write prose that is understandable, readable and interesting to the reader. A slight familiarity with archaeological literature will suggest that some writers do not bother to try. The result can be publications that even students of the discipline find incomprehensible, except for some who mistakenly conclude that this must be the required way to do things and attempt to imitate it in their own work.

Closely associated with other social sciences, archaeology is one of the principal means of investigating changes in human societies through time, particularly for pre-literate societies and undocumented aspects of literate ones. It provides a time-depth and an orientation largely denied to cultural or social anthropology and sociology. However, unlike historians, whose task in explaining the recorded past is to turn written documents or oral tradition into text, archaeologists have to turn physical evidence consisting of things and their contexts into text (although sometimes aided by documentary sources for later periods). Furthermore, except in the most specialized technical writing, that physical evidence has to be translated into text that is informative about people in the past and relevant to people in the present. This means that archaeological writing has to address special problems that arise from the character of its data, in addition to explaining its interpretations within the general context of the social sciences. Binford (1988: 19–20) suggested that we 'think of archaeological facts as a sort of untranslated language, something that we need to "decode" in order to move from simple statements about matter and its arrangement to statements of behavioral interest about the past'. The varied and frequently complex contributions of the natural sciences to archaeological investigations can make this task especially difficult, but the process of decryption involves not only interpretation of the evidence but also the presentation of the outcome in clearly written prose. Illustrations of many types, as well as tables, can contribute to this writing, providing visual explanation and relieving the text of some of the more burdensome details. However, illustrations and tables need to be closely integrated with that text, rather than merely used as cosmetic additions as is sometimes the case. Their photographic or graphic quality, their comprehensibility, their content, their sizes, their location within the text and their captions will all need very careful attention if they are to assist effectively in the task of writing.

Writing archaeology for publication is a skill that has to be learned. Acquiring proficiency is not a magical outcome of writing a doctoral thesis as some people seem to think, although the discipline of producing such a large formal text can certainly provide an initial apprenticeship. Basically, learning to write is rather like learning to ride a bicycle; one has to maintain a delicate balance whilst still moving forward, but at first one will frequently fall off, sometimes with painful results. When this happens, it is essential to try again immediately, even though writing, like riding a bicycle, can often result in little more than a sore bum. In short, one way to learn how to write is to write. Writing has to become a habit, with a strictly disciplined routine. Repeated attempts, in as wide a variety of formats as possible, will in time make the task easier for most people and, it is hoped, improve the quality of the product. In the process, one has to develop an objective critical approach to what has been written, attempting to read it as if someone else wrote it. Nevertheless, it is important not to be too critical. Many years ago, when an architectural historian friend of mine had laboured for several days writing a paper, I asked him how he was getting on. 'Nearly finished' was the reply, to which I remarked that he had done well to write a paper so quickly. 'No', he exclaimed, 'I have not nearly finished the paper; I have nearly finished the first paragraph'! Self-criticism is all very well, providing that it does not become self-destructive perfectionism. To quote a favourite maxim of Thurstan Shaw's: 'The better is often the enemy of the good'.

Another way to learn how to write about archaeology is to read what others have written, and to read as widely as possible amongst both archaeological and non-archaeological literature. Such reading should also range through time, certainly over the last two centuries and perhaps earlier. The important thing to observe is not only the content but also the manner in which it has been presented: the structure and style, particularly the way the prose flows or fails to do so, the way that descriptive material has been handled, the choice of words, the presence or absence of clarity. If you can understand what some authors have done that made them successful and what others have done or not done that detracted from the quality of their writing, then you can more readily appreciate the strengths and weaknesses of your own writing. This is not to suggest that you should imitate the way in which others have written, but you should certainly be prepared to learn from them. As Leonardo da Vinci stated in his view of science, 'Experience has been the mistress of whoever has written well' (Richter 1952: 2).

This book was written at the suggestion of Simon Whitmore, formerly a commissioning editor with Cambridge University Press. It resulted from an informal discussion that the two of us had at the 2005 York conference of the (American) Society for Historical Archaeology. I had stated that, unlike many archaeologists, I actually enjoyed writing, mainly because it is so difficult to do well and because the attempt to meet that challenge is stimulating in itself. I think that we both agonized about what Brian Fagan (2006a: 17), with enviable directness, has subsequently called 'the generally appalling standards of writing in archaeology'. In any event, the outcome was that I found myself trying to write a book that tells other people how to write about archaeology. This I regard as a virtually impossible task, as well as being conceptually arrogant. I also felt poorly qualified to write anything that looked like a methodological manual. Instead, I have written a book that reflects my own experiences of writing about archaeology (on related themes see Connah 2001b, 2004b, 2004c). It presents a personal view intended to be read, rather than a reference work intended to be consulted.

On the overall craft of writing there are, of course, many books, but compared to the large literature on the writing of history (Berger, Feldner and Passmore 2003 is an example), there appears to have been little written about the writing of archaeology. Indeed, in his admirable recent book, *Writing archaeology: Telling stories about the past*, Brian Fagan comments, 'There is almost no directly relevant literature' on this subject (Fagan 2006a: 168). Fagan does, in fact, provide a 'how to do it' book, but he concentrates on the writing of commercial general interest books, what he calls 'trade books', an area of publication in which he has been remarkably successful. My intention has been to cast my net very much wider, to encompass as much of the spectrum of archaeological writing as possible.

I have been aided in this task by the opinions of other archaeologists. Hodder (1989), for instance, has rightly argued that a more critical attention should be given to archaeological writing and has suggested that rhetoric, narrative and dialogue need more emphasis in such writing. Taking up these ideas, Joyce et al. (2002) have delved deeply into the theoretical aspects of archaeological writing, stressing what they perceive to be a need for innovation and experimentation. In addition, Joyce (2006) has written specifically about the writing of historical archaeology, and several papers on the theme of writing archaeology occupy most of an issue of the *Archaeological Review from Cambridge* (Writing archaeology 1989). Amongst other contributions on the subject of archaeological writing is that of Chippindale (1996), who has provided an interesting analysis of a paper of his own, identifying different 'moods' of writing that reflect different kinds of knowledge that it was hoped to convey. There is also a paper by Pluciennik (1999), with comments by others, that examines the role of narrative in archaeological writing. Furthermore, Betty

(2002) has provided a publisher's view of archaeological writing, and Jones et al. (2001) have contributed a useful survey concerning the publication of archaeological projects. As well as these sources, there is a general guide to scholarly publishing (Derricourt 1996a, 1996b) that deserves particular attention by archaeological writers because its author was an academic archaeologist before he became a publisher.

In addition to these varied published sources, I also hoped to gather a range of opinion in the form of personal communications from a selection of colleagues who had substantial experience of writing for publication. My optimism was not justified; a total of twenty-two written requests for comments on the subject produced only two responses. Apparently, writing about archaeology was not considered to be a matter of importance, or perhaps it was feared that I would quote what they had to say. However, Merrick Posnansky did respond and expressed the opinion that standards of archaeological writing had declined in recent decades, whereas Alasdair Brooks admired some of the work of James Deetz and Ivor Nöel Hume and contrasted it with the 'near-impenetrability and insomnia-curing prose' that now characterizes much archaeological writing.

It would appear that the nuts and bolts of writing about archaeology do deserve more attention than they are sometimes given. Therefore, my aim in this book is to help other archaeologists to write for publication and perhaps to write better than they might otherwise do. This goal might appear patronizing, but it is not intended to be. Inevitably, the book reflects my own personal views, rather than attempting to establish 'right' and 'wrong' ways of doing things. I neither regard my own writing as faultless, nor what I have to suggest as the only way of going about the job. After many years of university teaching and supervision, I am acutely aware that to some extent we all think differently and what works for one person might not work for another. This can be especially true for writers of diverse cultural backgrounds for whom English is a second language, particularly those from Africa and parts of Asia. For this reason the book has been written with the expectation that the reader might accept or reject its suggestions about the writing process, assuming that at least she or he will have been encouraged to think about that process, just as I have had to do in my own case. Naturally, the book raises theoretical issues, some of which are discussed, but the main orientation is a practical one. The book is principally intended for a readership of both academic and commercial professional archaeologists, as well as for students of archaeology, and heritage managers, but I hope it will interest anyone who writes about archaeology for whatever audience. As there is no point in writing books unless someone actually reads them, particular attention is given to the difficulties of writing in an interesting and readable manner.

The purpose of archaeological writing is to make the results of our investigations widely available, primarily to other archaeologists and scholars in related disciplines but also to society in general or to specific sections of it. This means publishing what we write, a process that includes a very wide range of printed formats, a growing body of digital outlets and, in the opinion of some people, even the so-called grey literature that has mushroomed in recent decades with the growth of archaeological consulting in much of the developed world. Therefore, the archaeological author needs to keep in mind the published form in which the writing will eventually appear. This means that, in addition to considering the craft of archaeological writing, it is also necessary to give close attention to the process of publication in its varied forms. Hence the emphasis in this book is on the archaeological author; the primary definition of the latter word in *The Concise Oxford Dictionary* is 'a writer, esp[ecially] of books', implying that an author is someone who writes specifically for publication (Allen 1990: 72).

As already indicated, there are many types of publications. Conventional printed hard copy is still very common and, for many authors, remains the most desirable form. Consisting of a mind-numbing variety of books and journals, from the most esoteric research items to those intended for general audiences, it is costly and slow to produce and often poorly distributed. The acquisition and shelving of copies also involve considerable expense for both libraries and individuals. Not surprisingly, some authors see digital publication on the Internet as the solution to these problems, but commercial publishers still have to charge for access and thoughtful readers inevitably wonder about information plasticity and archival sustainability. For example,

one can read a book printed in 1908 and know that one is reading exactly what was published at that time, but will people in
2108 be able to read a book published in a digital form in 2008
with the same assurance? Will there even be compatible hard-
ware and software available? As the head of the British Library
has warned, 'We are in danger of creating a black hole for future
historians and writers' (Brindley 2009), and consequently there
has been increasing concern about the preservation of digital
material (Borghoff et al. 2005; Harvey 2005; Pearson and Webb
2008). Finally, there is the grey literature, the enormous number
of printed (usually photocopied) reports produced by consulting
archaeologists. The problem here is availability: very few copies,
a restricted circulation (in some cases limited by the client or
by cultural sensitivity) and consequently a huge amount of data
that is not usually accessible for general reading. Arguably, grey
literature does not constitute publication at all.

Clearly, the archaeological writer has to select a publication
outlet with care and is more likely to have material accepted if
it has been written with that particular outlet in mind. Before
even starting to write, it is important to decide what the purpose
of the writing is and who are most likely to read it. The variety
of publication outlets and readerships for archaeological writing
is considerable, and the archaeological author needs to develop
an equally varied range of styles. Inevitably there will often be
a tension between the requirement for scientific rigour and the
necessity to produce interesting readable prose, which for more
general publication has also to be in a commercially viable form.
As might be expected of a discipline that straddles the humanities
and the sciences, those of us who attempt to write about it will
have to tackle many problems. The next chapter will consider
how other archaeologists, past and present, have addressed these
problems when writing about the past.

Two

Learning from others

Archaeological writers past and present

To understand archaeology, one needs to understand its history. Only by tracing the origins and development of the subject can one really appreciate how it has arrived at its present condition. This applies to archaeological writing just as it does to other aspects of the discipline. Braidwood (1981: 25) recalled with dismay how during the 'New Archaeology' of the 1960s and 1970s it was 'declared publicly' that 'nothing written before 1960 is worth reading'. Such an attitude is hardly helpful to the aspiring archaeological author. As already suggested in Chapter 1, one way to learn how to write, or to write more effectively, is to read widely and critically amongst the published literature of the relevant field. Older publications that handle data and theory in a manner now thought outdated can still be informative about the mechanics of writing and about stylistic treatment. More importantly, with the benefit of hindsight one can begin to understand how underpinning theories, the availability of data, the author's cultural background and the purpose of the publication have shaped the genre of writing that resulted. Furthermore, a wide knowledge of archaeological literature can reduce the risk of 'reinventing the wheel', a trap into which the writers of post-graduate theses occasionally fall but that must be avoided in publications. Indeed, it is also the case that 'connections and insights often result from reading about research in another field than one's own' (*Antiquaries Journal* 2008). In short, to be able to write well about archaeology, it is necessary to read what others have written about it and to think about what they have written. In doing this, one should recollect the warning by Chippindale (1989: 21–25) that much of the history of archaeology is the story of 'who was right in the past' according to our present under-standing of the discipline. At times we should also be prepared to consider the writings of some of those who have since been judged to be wrong. We should be wary of merely using the history of archaeology as a means of justifying ideas that happen to be current at the present time.

Early archaeological writing

The word 'archaeology' has been used in different ways over the last few centuries, and it is therefore difficult to decide at what point in time one can first identify archaeological writing in English. Perhaps the most appropriate place is with the English antiquaries of the sixteenth to eighteenth centuries, who repre-sented what Glyn Daniel (1967: 34) called 'a groping towards archaeology'. One of the earliest of these was William Cam-den, who in 1586 published a guide to British antiquities called *Britannia*. Originally written in Latin, it was translated into English by Philemon Holland in 1657 (Daniel 1976: 2). Here is part of a description of Silbury Hill, a well-known prehistoric mound in southern England:

> Here Selbury, a round hill, riseth to a considerable height, and seemeth by the fashion of it, and by the sliding down of the earth about it, to be cast up by men's hands. Of this sort there are many to be seen in this County, round and copped, which are call'd Burrows or Barrows, perhaps raised in memory of the Soldiers there slain. For bones are found in them; and I have read that it was a custom among the Northern People, that every soldier escaping alive out of Battel, was to bring his Helmet full of earth toward the raising of Monuments for their slain Fellows. Tho' I

rather think this Selbury-hill to be placed instead of a boundary,
if not by the Romans, yet by the Saxons, as well as the ditch call'd
Wodensdike, ... (Daniel 1967: 36)

In this passage some of the basic characteristics of archaeological writing can already be seen. There is the observation of a
piece of physical evidence and a deduction from that observation. This deduction is then set in the context of more general but
related physical evidence. An explanation is then sought in the
available literature, but this is dismissed in favour of the author's
more practical interpretation. These characteristics are apparent
in spite of somewhat archaic language. Also notable, in the first
edition of Camden's book, was an illustration of a Saxon chancel
arch, which has been claimed as the first illustration in an English
archaeological work (Daniel 1967: 36). It was the beginning of
what was to become a heavy reliance by archaeologists on the
visual presentation of material culture. In a manner less common amongst historians, pictures (in the broadest sense) were to
become an integral part of archaeological writing.

Another of the early English antiquaries whose importance
has been stressed by historians of archaeology was John Aubrey
(Hunter 1975). His *An Essay towards the description of the North
Division of Wiltshire*, written between 1659 and 1670, includes
the following passage:

> Let us imagine then what kind of countrie this was in the time
> of the Ancient Britons. By the nature of the soil, which is a sour
> woodsere land, very natural for the production of akes especially,
> one may conclude that this North Division was a shady dismal
> wood; and the inhabitants almost as savage as the Beasts whose
> skins were their only rayment. . . . The Boats of the Avon (which
> signifies River) were basketts of twigges covered with an oxe skin;
> which the poore people in Wales use to this day. They call them
> curricles. (Daniel 1967: 37–38)

Here again are attributes that have long characterized archaeological writing: a concern to show how it was in the past, in this
case attempting to reconstruct its environment, and also the use
of ethnographic observation to flesh out the narrative.

However, perhaps the most remarkable of those who wrote
about archaeology during this period was William Stukeley,
a curiously eccentric man who was nevertheless an accurate

observer in the field (Piggott 1950). He was, for instance, the first to provide clear descriptions of cropmarks, although John Leland, William Camden, John Aubrey and Thomas Hearne had individually recorded their presence previously. The manner in which the differential growth of vegetation can reveal buried archaeological features was to become important for aerial photographers in the early twentieth century, but Stukeley had already provided a succinctly written account two hundred years earlier in 1725, in his *Itinerarium Curiosum*. At Great Chesterford, in Essex, he made the following observation:

> In the North-West end of the city, the people promised to show me a wonderful thing in the corn, which they observed every year with some sort of superstition. I found it to be the foundation of a Roman temple very apparent, it being almost harvest time. Here the poverty of the corn growing where the walls stood, defines it to such a nicety that I was able to measure it with exactness enough. (Fagan 1959: 280)

In spite of what Daniel (1967: 44) called his 'Druidomania', it is apparent that Stukeley could write about field archaeology in a concise and straightforward manner and that he was already using local informants as many later archaeologists were to do.

A concern for context, particularly stratigraphic context, has long been a major theme in archaeological writing. A famous early example was the letter written by John Frere in 1797 that was published by the Society of Antiquaries of London in its journal *Archaeologia* in 1800. Although Frere's letter was subsequently forgotten for a half-century, it has since become regarded as an important step in the development of archaeology. Frere had found flint artefacts of the sort that later became known as Acheulean handaxes; they were with the bones of unknown animals at a depth of about 4 metres in a brick pit at Hoxne, in Suffolk. They lay in gravel that had been covered in turn by sand, clay and humus. After describing the stratification, Frere wrote:

> The situation in which these weapons were found may tempt us to refer them to a very remote period indeed; even before that of the present world; but, whatever our conjectures on that head may

be, it will be difficult to account for the stratum in which they lie being covered with another stratum, which, on that supposition, may be conjectured to have been once the bottom, or at least the shore, of the sea. The manner in which they lie would lead to the persuasion that it was a place of their manufacture and not of their accidental deposit; and the numbers of them were so great that the man who carried on the brick-work told me that, before he was aware of their being objects of curiosity, he had emptied baskets full of them into the ruts of the adjoining road. (Frere 1800: 205)

Frere's logical treatment of the evidence and the clarity of his interpretation and its written expression are, indeed, remarkable when one recollects that he wrote before the establishment of the antiquity of humanity and the acceptance of the idea of prehistory that came about more than fifty years later. Furthermore, his published letter was accompanied by full-sized illustrations of two of the handaxes, in both face and side view (Frere 1800: Plates XIV & XV). Apparently the work of a professional engraver, these illustrations are creditable efforts even by modern standards and are good early examples of visual material supporting the text.

The stratigraphic context of the stone artefacts at Hoxne was revealed by the commercial digging of clay for brick making, but formal excavation for the purpose of recovering ancient artefacts and information about the people who made them was already being undertaken elsewhere. Describing the results of such work was to become a major part of archaeological writing, a notable early example being the account by Thomas Jefferson, the third president of the United States, of his 1784 excavation of a burial mound in Virginia. His purpose was to discover which of the theories about such mounds was correct:

I proceeded then to make a perpendicular cut through the body of the barrow, that I might examine its internal structure. This passed about three feet from its center, was opened to the former surface of the earth, and was wide enough for a man to walk through and examine its sides. At the bottom, that is, on the level of the circumjacent plain, I found bones; above these a few stones, brought from a cliff a quarter of a mile off, and from the river one-eighth of a mile off; then a large interval of earth, then a stratum of bones, and so on. At one end of the section were four strata of bones plainly distinguishable; at the other, three; the strata in one part not ranging with those in another. The bones nearest the surface were least decayed. No holes were discovered in any of them, as if made with bullets, arrows, or other weapons. I conjectured that in this barrow might have been a thousand skeletons. Every one will readily seize the circumstances above related, which militate against the opinion, that it covered the bones only of persons fallen in battle; and against the tradition also, which would make it the common sepulchre of a town, in which the bodies were placed upright, and touching each other. Appearances certainly indicate that it has derived both origin and growth from the accustomary collection of bones, and deposition of them together; that the first collection had been deposited on the common surface of the earth, a few stones put over it, and then a covering of earth, that the second had been laid on this, had covered more or less of it in proportion to the number of bones, and was then also covered with earth; and so on. The following are the particular circumstances which give it this aspect. 1. The number of bones. 2. Their confused position. 3. Their being in different strata. 4. The strata in one part have no correspondence with those in another. 5. The different states of decay in these strata, which seem to indicate a difference in the time of inhumation. 6. The existence of infant bones among them. (Jefferson 1955 [1787]: 99–100)

This account of complex excavated evidence and its interpretation has been described as 'characteristic of his [Jefferson's] inquiring and scientific attitude of mind' (Chamberlain 1907: 499), and it achieves a clarity that is impressive. The rather heavy prose is controlled by careful punctuation, and the numbered summary at the end ties things together nicely.

The writing about archaeological matters discussed so far was by scholarly antiquarians and members of the elite, in both cases writing about the antiquities of their own countries and writing for people similar to them. However, there was also an interest in the remains of Ancient Greece and Rome, and during the nineteenth century this interest extended to many other exotic past societies, particularly to that of Pharaonic Egypt. These subjects developed a mass appeal; an increasingly literate English-speaking people were fascinated by writings about former 'civilizations' that had flourished and then disappeared.

Museums and private collectors developed insatiable appetites for antiquities from these sources; investigators and adventurers profited from their acquisition and from written accounts of how this was accomplished. One of the most outrageous of these individuals was Giovanni Battista Belzoni, circus strongman, salesman, and tomb robber, whose exploits in Egypt in the early nineteenth century were written up in a style that would have made Hollywood's Indiana Jones envious. Belzoni was Italian, but his *Narrative of the operations and recent discoveries within the pyramids, temples, tombs, and excavations, in Egypt and Nubia*, published in 1820, was written in English. The following is a brief sample of his account of Egyptian tomb robbing:

> Of some of these tombs many persons could not withstand the suffocating air, which often causes fainting. A vast quantity of dust rises, so fine that it enters into the throat and nostrils, and chokes the nose and mouth to such a degree, that it requires great power of lungs to resist it and the strong effluvia of the mummies. This is not all; the entry or passage where the bodies are is roughly cut in the rocks, and the falling of the sand from the upper part or ceiling of the passage causes it to be nearly filled up. In some places there is not more than a vacancy of a foot left, which you must contrive to pass through in a creeping posture like a snail, on pointed and keen stones, that cut like glass. After getting through these passages, some of them two or three hundred yards long, you generally find a more commodious place, perhaps high enough to sit. But what a place of rest! surrounded by bodies, by heaps of mummies in all directions; which, previous to my being accustomed to the sight, impressed me with horror. The blackness of the wall, the faint light given by the candles or torches for want of air, the different objects that surrounded me, seeming to converse with each other, and the Arabs with the candles or torches in their hands, naked and covered with dust, themselves resembling living mummies, absolutely formed a scene that cannot be described. In such a situation I found myself several times, and often returned exhausted and fainting, till at last I became inured to it, and indifferent to what I suffered, except from the dust, which never failed to choke my throat and nose; and though, fortunately, I am destitute of the sense of smelling, I could taste that the mummies were rather unpleasant to swallow. (Belzoni 1971 [1820]: 156–157)

This prose is as breathless as Belzoni must have been while exploring such tombs, and one can imagine its impact on polite readers in England. Partly this effect results from the subject matter, but it is heightened by the length of some sentences; for example, the final one has sixty-four words, and he managed to squeeze ninety-three words into a sentence in another passage (Belzoni 1971 [1820]: 259). However, Belzoni came to a miserable end, dying in 1823 at the age of forty-five in Gwato, on the coast of what is now Nigeria, one of the many European victims of West African exploration (Roth 1903: 3).

The development of observational writing

It was a characteristic of early archaeology that the more prolific and sophisticated the surviving material evidence for a past society, the less the care that was taken with its recovery and study. Conversely, where the evidence was limited, a greater effort had to be made to extract information from it. In contrast to Belzoni's depredations, some of the numerous barrow diggers of early-nineteenth-century England did, at times, try to be more careful. Here is part of an account by Thomas Bateman (Marsden 2007) of the excavation of a prehistoric burial mound on Middleton Moor in 1848:

> Fortunately the contents, with the exception of one skeleton that lay near the surface, had been enclosed in a cist, sunk a few inches beneath the level of the soil. As in the companion barrow, the skeleton near the top was dismembered by the plough, so that it afforded nothing worthy of notice – the original interment, however, which lay rather deeper, in a kind of rude cist or enclosure, formed by ten shapeless masses of limestone, amply repaid our labour. The persons thus interred consisted of a female in the prime of life, and a child of about four years of age; the former had been placed on the floor of the grave on her left side, with the knees drawn up; the child was placed above her, and rather behind her shoulders: they were surrounded and covered with innumerable bones of the water-vole, or rat, and near the woman was a cow's tooth, an article uniformly found with the more ancient interments. Round her neck was a necklace of variously shaped beads and other trinkets of jet and bone, curiously

ornamented, upon the whole resembling those found at Cow Low in 1846 . . . but differing from them in many details. The various pieces of this compound ornament are 420 in number, which unusual quantity is accounted for by the fact of 348 of the beads being thin laminae only; 54 are of cylindrical form, and the 18 remaining pieces are conical studs and perforated plates, the latter in some cases ornamented with punctured patterns. Altogether, the necklace is the most elaborate production of the pre-metallic period that I have seen. (Bateman 1861: 24–26)

This brief but detailed account was accompanied by two engravings, one of the restrung necklace and one of the female skeleton *in situ* but considerably idealized. In the preface of his book, *Ten years' diggings in Celtic and Saxon grave hills, in the counties of Derby, Stafford, and York, from 1848 to 1858* . . . , Bateman wrote:

I will only add, that theory, the bane of nearly all the older Antiquarian books, has been avoided, and that the very few deductions that I have ventured to make from recorded facts are either demonstrable, or such as may be fairly inferred. (Bateman 1861: vi)

This was an early example of the minimal interpretation that was to characterize so much archaeological writing for the next hundred years or more. Indeed, the extent to which inference from archaeological data is justifiable remains an issue for archaeological writers.

By the time Bateman's book was published, ideas in Europe about the ancient past were changing. The acceptance by John Evans and Joseph Prestwich of Jacques Boucher de Perthes's evidence for the antiquity of humanity occurred in the year 1859, as did the publication of Darwin's *Origin of species*. These events have often been regarded as a watershed in the development of archaeology (Daniel 1975), one of the earliest outcomes being John Lubbock's book *Pre-historic times, as illustrated by ancient remains and the manners and customs of modern savages*. It was published in London in 1865. In spite of a tendency to digress and to be data-heavy, this is a book that is innovative, logical and clearly written. It also contains high-quality engravings and tables, the latter introduced in the second edition of 1869, which

is the source of the following quotation. Here is a crucial passage
in which the author sums up the evidence for the basic techno-
logical sequence, on which European prehistory was to depend
until the middle of the twentieth century:

> From these and similar discoveries, it appears evident that the use
> of bronze weapons had been discontinued in the North before,
> probably long before, the commencement of our era. From the
> ease with which bronze could be worked, this metal was still used
> for brooches and ornaments; but in the manufacture of swords,
> axes, and similar implements, it had been entirely superseded by
> iron. There are many cases on record of iron swords with bronze
> handles or scabbards, but scarcely an instance of the reverse.
>
> Conversely, as bronze weapons are entirely absent from the great
> "finds" of the Iron Age, so are iron weapons altogether wanting
> in those instances where . . . large quantities of bronze tools and
> weapons have been found together.
>
> To sum up this argument, though the discoveries of bronze and
> of iron weapons have been very numerous, yet there is hardly
> a single case in which swords, axes, daggers, or other weapons
> of these two different metals have been found together; nor are
> bronze weapons found associated with inscriptions, or with coins,
> pottery, or other relics of Roman origin.
>
> So, also, though no doubt stone weapons were used during the
> Bronze Age, there are many cases in which large numbers of stone
> implements and weapons have been found without any of metal.
> (Lubbock 1869: 12)

Lubbock's book was widely read and went through seven editions, the last one being published in 1913, having been revised
by him shortly before his death (Daniel 1967: 122). That a book
could remain in print for a half-century suggests that the author
did his work well.

However, while prehistoric archaeology in Europe was replac-
ing the fundamentalist biblical account of the remote past, excavators in what is now Iraq were providing support for other
parts of the Bible. The most notable of these was Austen Henry
Layard, whose book *Nineveh and its remains*, published in 1849,
was an instant popular success and was described as 'the most
extraordinary work of the present age' (Reade 1998: 913). Apart
from the biblical associations, it seems to have been the exotic

subject and Layard's fluent style of writing that attracted readers, who could also see for themselves some of his great discoveries displayed in the British Museum. An idea of the scale of his activities and of the way that he wrote about them can be gained from the following passage about his excavations at Kuyunjik (eventually identified as Nineveh) in his 1853 book *Discoveries in the ruins of Nineveh and Babylon*:

> Such were the discoveries in the ruined palace of Sennacherib at the time of my departure for Europe. In this magnificent edifice I had opened no less than seventy-one halls, chambers, and passages, whose walls, almost without an exception, had been panelled with slabs of sculptured alabaster recording the wars, the triumphs, and the great deeds of the Assyrian king. By a rough calculation, about 9880 feet, or nearly two miles, of bas-reliefs, with twenty-seven portals, formed by colossal winged bulls and lion-sphinxes, were uncovered in that part alone of the building explored during my researches. The greatest length of the excavations was about 720 feet, the greatest breadth about 600 feet. The pavement of the chambers was from 20 to 35 feet below the surface of the mound. (Layard 1853: 589)

These achievements need to be considered in the context of Layard's deplorable excavation techniques, 'which consisted of tunnelling along the base of the walls' where sculptures might be found (Lloyd 1955: 154). Indeed, at the site of Qal'at Sharqât he failed to find any structures at all because he cut through mud-brick walls without recognizing them (Lloyd 1955: 148). In addition, Layard was not immune to a common weakness in archaeological writing that might be called the laundry-list approach. The following is from his 1853 book:

> Other devices found among these impressions of seals are: – 1. A king, attended by a priest, in act of adoration before a deity standing on a lion, and surrounded by seven stars: above the god's head, on one seal, is a scorpion. 2. The king, followed by an attendant bearing a parasol, and preceded by a rampant horse. 3. A god, or the king, probably the former, rising from a crescent. There appears to be a fish in front of the figure. 4. The king, with a eunuch or priest before him; a flower, or ornamented staff, between them. 5. A scorpion, surrounded by a guilloche border (a device of very frequent occurrence, and probably astronomical). 6. A priest worshipping before a god, encircled by stars. 7. A

priest worshipping before a god. Behind him are a bull, and the sacred astronomical emblems. 8. An ear of corn, surrounded by a fancy border. 9. An object resembling a dagger, with flowers attached to the handle; perhaps a sacrificial knife. 10. The head of a bull and a trident, two sacred symbols of frequent occurrence on Assyrian monuments. 11. A crescent in the midst of a many-rayed star. 12. Several rudely cut seals, representing priests and various sacred animals, stars, &c. (Layard 1853: 154–155)

It is regrettable that archaeologists have so often found it necessary to write in this way; it is unbelievable that they have expected anyone to read what they have written.

Not surprisingly, other nineteenth-century archaeological pioneers were more concerned with the credibility of their subject in the academic world. Attention began to focus on methods of fieldwork and excavation, on the theory of data analysis, on the limits of interpretation and on the requirements of scientific publication. One of the most notable exponents of this new approach was Englishman Lieutenant-General Augustus Henry Lane Fox Pitt Rivers, generally referred to as Pitt Rivers (Thompson 1977). He is now principally remembered for his contributions to excavation technique, largely because of the promotion of his work by Mortimer Wheeler during the twentieth century, who called him 'the greatest of all archaeological excavators' (Wheeler 1954: v). However, it is the exceptional quality of the publication of his excavations that enables us to appreciate these achievements. For instance, his section of Bokerly Dyke, drawn between 1888 and 1891 (Pitt Rivers 1892: Plate CLXIII), makes the work of many later excavators look poor in comparison. Nevertheless, Pitt Rivers was more than just a disciplined excavator and rigorous publisher of his excavations; he also wrote on ethnological subjects and was particularly interested in the evolution of culture. The following example of his style is taken from an 1874 paper 'On early modes of navigation', published under the name of A. Lane Fox in 1875:

> Here, in the Nydam Moss, in Slesvic, in 1863, was discovered a large boat, seventy-seven feet long, ten feet ten inches broad in the middle, flat at the bottom, but higher and sharper at both ends, having a prow at both ends, like those described by Tacitus as having been built by the Suiones, who inhabited this country and Sweden in ancient times. This vessel, from its associated remains,

has been attributed to the third century [AD]. The bottom consisted of a broad plank, about two feet broad in the middle, but diminishing in width towards each end. A small keel, eight inches broad and one deep, was carved on the under side of the plank, which corresponds to the bottom plank, which, in Africa and the Polynesian Islands, we have shown to be the vestige of the dug-out trunk. On to this bottom plank, five side planks, running the whole length of the vessel, were built, but they differed from those previously described in overlapping, being clinker-built, and attached to each other, not by strings or wooden pins, but by large iron bolts. The planks, however, resembled those of the southern hemisphere, in having clamps or ledges carved out of the solid on the inside; these ledges were perforated, and their position corresponded to rows of vertical ribs, to which, like the vessels at Ké Island, and elsewhere in the Pacific, they were *tied* by means of cords passing through corresponding holes in the ribs. Each rib was carved out of one piece, and, like those of Ké Island, in the Asiatic Archipelago, could easily have been taken out and replaced by others after the vessel was completed. (Fox 1875: 418–419)

This is a successful description of a complicated arrangement, and it was achieved without the aid of illustrations.

Another English archaeologist who has been credited with methodological and theoretical innovation was William Matthew Flinders Petrie, whose archaeological activities continued for so long that he was able to entitle his 1932 autobiography *Seventy years in archaeology* (his protégé, Margaret Murray, outdid this in 1963 by calling hers *My first hundred years*). His middle names acknowledged his grandfather Matthew Flinders, explorer and surveyor of the Australian coastline. Like Flinders, Petrie was clearly determined to achieve great things. It has been claimed that Petrie 'transformed Egyptology', putting it 'on a fully scientific basis' (Silverberg 1985: 46), but according to Wheeler (1954: 15): 'between the technical standards of Petrie and those of his older contemporary Pitt Rivers, there yawned a gulf into which two generations of Near Eastern archaeologists have in fact plunged to destruction'. Nevertheless, archaeology demands scholarship as well as methodological skills, and there have been few people who have excelled in both areas. In Petrie's case, whatever his technical ability, there is no doubt about the scholarly endeavour of his ninety-seven books. The following extract, which forms part of a discussion of the Great Pyramid of Khufu, at Giza, comes from his 1894 *History of Egypt*, Volume I, and provides a fitting example of his interests and writing skills:

> The pyramid was built of stone from the quarries on the opposite side of the Nile; both the fine casing and the rough core must have come from there, as no such stone, and no equivalent quarries, exist on the west bank. The tradition recorded by Herodotus as to the labour employed, is so entirely reasonable for the execution of such a work, that we cannot hesitate to accept it. It is said that a hundred thousand men were levied for three months at a time (*i.e.* during the three months of the inundation, when ordinary labour is at a standstill); and on this scale the pyramid-building occupied twenty years. On reckoning the number and weight of stones, this labour would fully suffice for the work. The skilled masons had large barracks, now behind the second pyramid, which might hold even four thousand men; but perhaps a thousand would suffice to do all the fine work in the time. Hence there was no impossibility in the task, and no detriment to the country in employing a small proportion of the population at a season when they were all idle by the compulsion of natural causes. The training and skill which they would acquire by such work would be a great benefit to the national character.
>
> The workmanship greatly varies in different parts. The entrance passage and the casing are perhaps the finest; the flatness and squareness of the joints being extraordinary, equal to opticians' work of the present day, but on a scale of acres instead of feet or yards of material. The squareness and level of the base is brilliantly true, the average error being less than a ten-thousandth of the side in equality, in squareness, and in level. (Petrie 1894: 39–40)

Even if Petrie's archaeology did compare unfavourably with the best work being done elsewhere, it was still a great improvement on previous activities in Egypt.

In spite of the increasing interest in method and theory by some archaeologists, there were still archaeological adventurers excited by the act of discovery itself. One such was the American Edward Herbert Thompson, whose exploration of the Sacred Well of Chichén Itzá in Mexico has been called 'one of the most remarkable exploits in archaeological annals' (Silverberg 1985: 317). The well is actually a deep, water-filled natural hole in the limestone plateau of Yucatan, one of many that are known as *cenotes*. Its maximum diameter is 187 feet (57 metres), and according to sixteenth-century Spanish accounts, it had been the local custom to throw into it both objects and people as sacrifices. Thompson decided to retrieve as much of this material as possible, first by using a dredge on a long cable from the cliff top up to 80 feet (24 metres) above the surface of the water, and then by actually diving in the pit itself. This was during 1904 to 1907, long before the development of free diving and at a time requiring the use of a diving suit equipped with a copper helmet, air hose, life-line, speaking tube, lead weights and iron-soled shoes. Diving was a dangerous business, even for professionals, but Thompson took lessons in deep-sea diving from an expert and became what he called 'a fairly good diver, but by no means a perfect one' (Thompson 1933: 269–270). Thus prepared, when the dredge eventually ceased to recover artefacts and bones, he began diving in the great pit, accompanied by a professional Greek diver. The following extract from his 1932 book (1933 edition) *People of the serpent* describes his first dive, to a depth of 60 to 80 feet (18 to 24 metres):

As I stepped on the first rung of the ladder, each of the pumping gang, my faithful native boys, left his place in turn and with a very solemn face shook hands with me and then went back again to wait for the signal. It was not hard to read their thoughts. They were bidding me a last farewell, never expecting to see me again. Then, releasing my hold on the ladder, I sank like a bag of lead, leaving behind me a silvery chain of bubbles.

During the first ten feet of descent, the light rays changed from yellow to green and then to a purplish black. After that I was in utter darkness. Sharp pains shot through my ears, because of the increasing air pressure. When I gulped and opened the air valves in my helmet a sound like "pht! pht!" came from each ear and then the pain ceased. Several times this process had to be repeated before I stood on the bottom. I noted another curious sensation on my way down. I felt as if I were rapidly losing weight until, as I stood on the flat end of a big stone column that had fallen from the old ruined shrine above, I seemed to have almost no weight at all. I fancied that I was more like a bubble than a man clogged by heavy weights.

But I felt as well a strange thrill when I realized that I was the only living being who had ever reached this place alive and expected to leave it again still living. Then the Greek diver came down beside me and we shook hands.

... The medium in which we had to work was neither water nor mud, but a combination of both, stirred up by the working of the dredge. It was a thick mixture like gruel and no ray so feeble as that of a flashlight could even penetrate it. (Thompson 1933: 281–282)

Thompson admitted to a legacy of 'injured ear drums and greatly impaired hearing' (Thompson 1933: 286), but he had proved the old traditions about the Sacred Well to be correct and had recovered a great many artefacts of jade, gold, copper and other materials, of Mayan and later date.

Archaeological writing comes of age

Soon after Thompson's exploits in the Chichén Itzá *cenote*, Alfred Vincent Kidder was beginning his pioneering archaeological investigations in the American Southwest. Kidder is credited with being the first archaeologist to make use of large-scale stratigraphic excavation in that region, having come under the influence of the noted Egyptologist G.A. Reisner while studying at Harvard (Willey and Sabloff 1980: 89). His excavations at Pecos, in New Mexico, were to make an important contribution to the development of archaeology in the United States. The following extract is from a 1917 paper of his, 'Prehistoric cultures of the San Juan drainage', that provided a synthesis of the archaeology of that area that has been called 'the first such summary for a major portion of the United States' (Woodbury 1973: 99). The extract provides a clearly written introduction to a major part of the cultural sequence of the American Southwest as it was then understood:

The earliest sedentary or at least agricultural inhabitants of whom we have knowledge were the so-called "Basket-makers". Discovered by the Wetherill brothers in the Grand Gulch region of southeastern Utah, the remains were first brought to the notice of archaeologists through papers by Mr. Pepper, describing collections made by the Wetherills and other professional diggers, and quoting statements made by them.

According to these accounts the "Basket-makers" occupied round subterranean rooms dug in the compact earth floors of the large caves that they always seemed to inhabit. They built cists, both plain and stone-lined – primarily for storage, secondarily for burial. The crania found in the graves were all undeformed and the bodies were always accompanied with baskets. Baskets indeed were evidently one of the chief products of the people, for they occurred in the caves in large numbers and of most excellent workmanship. Pottery vessels, on the other hand, were scarce and crude, and usually bore on their bottoms the imprint of the baskets in which they had been formed. Also characteristic of the culture was the use of the atlatl, or throwing stick, and the weaving of peculiar square-toed sandals. It was definitely stated by the Wetherills that these remains were often found underneath typical stone cliff-dwellings. The range of the culture was given as Grand Gulch, the adjoining cañons, and possibly the Cañon de Chelly. (Woodbury 1973: 100)

Kidder lived from 1885 to 1963, a period during which American archaeology made great progress, to which his work in both the Southwest and in Mexico contributed significantly.

In Europe, as excavations particularly of prehistoric sites continued to produce more and more data, the writing of archaeological syntheses became increasingly common. One of the most important authors of these was Vere Gordon Childe, who between 1915 and 1956 produced more than 280 publications, of which some 18 were single-authored books (Smith 1955). Childe was an academic working in Britain, whose left-wing opinions had excluded him from university employment in his native Australia. Nevertheless, his conventional training in classics and ancient history at the University of Sydney seems to have persuaded him that cultural diffusion from southwest Asia and the eastern Mediterranean was the major factor in European prehistory. His writings were immensely influential, although sometimes not very readable, one of the most significant being *The dawn of European civilization*, first published in 1925 and followed by other editions until 1957. The following passage from its second (1927) edition provides a sample of his interpretations and his style:

It must then be admitted that true civilizations had grown up and were well established in the Ancient East while Europe was still sunk in epipalaeolithic barbarism. The well-known identity between the earliest domestic animals and cultivated plants of Europe and Asia is therefore a valid argument for the view that the gifts that distinguish the neolithic culture from the palae-olithic, came to Europe from the Ancient East. The true origi-nality of our ancestors was displayed not in inventing what early climatic conditions had reserved for others, but in the manner in which they adapted and improved the inventions of the Orient. In this sense the early inhabitants of our continent were truly and remarkably creative and before the end of the second millennium had outstripped their masters and created an individual civiliza-tion of their own. But it was not the fruit of a miraculous birth, but the result of the diffusion and adaptation of the discoveries of the Orient and it is that which we must trace in this book. (Childe 1927: 23–24)

Perhaps this passage is an unfair example of Childe's writings, which in both their breadth and detail displayed remarkable scholarship that still attracts readers, outdated though many of the interpretations are. Nevertheless, as a student in the 1950s, I did feel that archaeology had to be something more than a procession of 'cultures' with names like Aunjetitz, Fatyanovo, Marschwitz and Michelsberg, and I was unconvinced by the travels of beakers that seemed to have grown legs and trotted around much of Western Europe. It needs to be remembered, however, that Childe's thinking was largely conditioned by the circumstances of the 1920s to 1940s. Before the impact of radio-carbon dating in the 1950s, there were few means of dating pre-historic communities in Western Europe, except by extending often-tenuous links to what Childe called 'the Ancient East'.

Indeed, as archaeological research extended into other parts of the world, the problems of chronology became even more severe. For example, the date of the construction of Great Zimbabwe, in southern central Africa, was the subject of serious dispute. It had been claimed to be the work of Semitic colonists three or four millennia ago; in contrast it was later attributed to ances-tors of the local Shona people during the first half of the second millennium AD. Excavations during 1929 by the Englishwoman Gertrude Caton-Thompson aimed to solve this problem. Sub-sequently, she was able 'to publish her evidence in its entirety with complete inventories and detailed descriptions of all her finds, however repetitive and mundane these might appear, and photographs of most of them' (Garlake 1973: 81). Her 1931 book, *The Zimbabwe culture: Ruins and reactions*, was a classic example of the monographic excavation reports that became a common form of archaeological writing during the twentieth century. She found the ruins to have been built by local people 'well within the Christian era' (Caton-Thompson 1931: 185); she also solved the mystery of the seemingly meaningless jumble of stone walls on some parts of the site:

> I have suggested that the cement floors and bevelled dais or benches are all that remain in the Maund [site] of the original huts; I believe the positions of these original huts to have been the same as those occupied later by the daga mounds – namely, positions intentionally forming the centre of short radial walls. The evidence for this is threefold. In the first place we noted, a significant fact, that the cement floors in those rare instances where they have escaped destruction within the periphery of the daga mounds, continue across the areas lying *between* ends of walls; this happens, for instance, between Walls 1–3 and 18, 21, 22, and it indicates forcibly enough that these short lengths of disconnected walls never linked, for their foundations are below the floor-level. They were disconnected from the day they were built. But supply a central structure of wood or daub – what you will – their idiotic isolation ceases; their detachment becomes intelligible. So sure am I that this is the true explanation of an otherwise senseless arrangement, that I have in our plan . . . superposed the visionary on the concrete and restored the circumferences of these vanished huts. The result is conclusive. (Caton-Thompson 1931: 56)

I have always regretted that I never met Caton-Thompson, who died at the age of ninety-seven in 1985; I think that she knew what she was doing.

A person whom I did meet on a number of occasions was the British archaeologist Mortimer Wheeler, a colourful character who was one of the most able excavators of his generation and the author of (amongst other things) the iconic excavation report *Maiden Castle, Dorset* published in 1943. This was a remarkable publication, particularly considering that it was published during World War II, in which Wheeler saw action, as he had in

World War I. In the book, a 'General Survey' was followed by detailed discussions of the 'Sites Excavated' and of the 'Finds', with an 'Epilogue' and 'Appendix' near the end of the 399 text pages. The book was of a large format and generously illustrated with excellent black-and-white photographs, which at that time had to be printed on glossy paper separate from the text. There were also many drawings including maps, plans, sections and artefacts, all of high quality. Wheeler himself signed some plans and sections, their excellence reflecting his early training at the Slade School of Fine Art in London (Hawkes 1982: 43–44). However, Wheeler's book was not just a presentation of material evidence. In his 1954 book *Archaeology from the earth*, he famously insisted that 'the archaeologist is digging up, not *things*, but *people*' (Wheeler 1954: v), and in his book on Maiden Castle there was a passage about the storming of this Iron Age hill fort by the Roman army that demonstrated this belief. A part of it follows:

> What happened there is plain to read. First, the regiment of artillery, which normally accompanied a legion on campaign, was ordered into action, and put down a barrage of iron-shod ballista-arrows over the eastern part of the site. Following this barrage, the infantry advanced up the slope, cutting its way from rampart to rampart, tower to tower. In the innermost bay of the entrance, close outside the actual gates, a number of huts had recently been built; these were now set alight, and under the rising clouds of smoke the gates were stormed and the position carried. But resistance had been obstinate and the fury of the attackers was roused. For a space, confusion and massacre dominated the scene. Men and women, young and old, were savagely cut down, before the legionaries were called to heel and the work of systematic destruction began. That work included the uprooting of some at least of the timbers which revetted the fighting-platform on the summit of the main rampart; but above all it consisted of the demolition of the gates and the overthrow of the high stone walls which flanked the two portals. The walls were now reduced to the lowly and ruinous state in which they were discovered by the excavator nearly nineteen centuries later.

> That night, when the fires of the legion shone out (we may imagine) in orderly lines across the valley, the survivors crept forth from their broken stronghold and, in the darkness, buried their dead as nearly as might be outside their tumbled gates, in that place where the ashes of their burned huts lay warm and thick

upon the ground. The task was carried out anxiously and hastily and without order, but, even so, from few graves were omitted those tributes of food and drink which were the proper and traditional perquisites of the dead. (Wheeler 1943: 62)

The imaginative reconstruction of events, of which this passage is a part, was then followed by a careful consideration of the evidence on which it was based.

Wheeler was one of the very small number of professional archaeologists in Britain before World War II, but a few years after that war the number of professionals began to grow substantially, in both Britain and America. At the same time a range of radiometric and other absolute dating techniques became available, freeing archaeologists from their previous fixation on chronology. The outcome was a period of questioning about the nature of archaeology and its objectives. This was mainly during the 1960s and 1970s, but Walter W. Taylor's 1948 book *A study of archeology* had already called for change. Taylor presented a damaging critique of Americanist archaeology as then practised and proposed the adoption of what he called 'the conjunctive approach', in which archaeological data were to be viewed as cultural data and history was to be written by the chronological construction of cultural contexts. Although at the time not well received by the archaeological establishment (Willey and Sabloff 1980: 139), Taylor's book was later to become almost a sacred text for the so-called New Archaeologists. The book is a closely argued theoretical study that has been described as 'not a particularly easy book' and one 'that makes serious demands on the reader' (Watson 1983: x). Nevertheless, I recently reread it, in its entirety, and was pleasantly surprised by the level of lucidity that the author was able to achieve in his prose, compared with the obscurity of much later theoretical writing by others. Here is Taylor addressing the thorny question of the appropriate level of interpretation in archaeological writing:

Empirical categories have their very specific place in archeological studies and reports, but they do not comprise, either singly or in the aggregate, what may properly be called a cultural context. This point will be treated at some length later in this chapter. Here it is sufficient to indicate that an archeological cultural context, by the very nature of the basic materials, is constructed by inference to a greater extent, perhaps, than contexts based on written or living sources. But there is no other means to construct them, and without contexts there is no way either to write history or to study culture. Therefore it behooves the archeologist not to maintain the untenable position of "sticking to the facts", meaning the renunciation of inference, hypothesis, and testing. It rather is incumbent upon him to derive his observational data as objectively as possible, to differentiate between observed fact and derived inference, to make explicitly labeled interpretations of as detailed and full a nature as possible, and then to look, either in the ground or among the data at hand, for evidence by which his hypotheses may be tested. Thus, more interpretation is called for, not less! If his readers find fault with his conclusions, they have but to examine the observational data and make their own inferences or set about producing, from the ground or elsewhere, more empirical evidence upon which to base alternative interpretations. (Taylor 1983: 114–115)

Six decades later, Taylor remains worth reading, although his assumption that archaeologists were necessarily male was not valid even at the time that he wrote.

In spite of focussing on Americanist archaeology, Taylor rather surprisingly commended the work of the British archaeologist Grahame Clark, describing him as 'one of the few archaeologists who has presented his material under broad cultural categories and written what, in effect, is an archeological ethnography' (Taylor 1983: 170). Such praise was amply justified, for it was Clark who from the 1930s onwards promoted an economic and ecological approach to the prehistoric past. Amongst his extensive writings were three editions of a world prehistory (Clark 1961, 1969, 1977), a synthesis that could not have been written before the availability of radiocarbon dates. Perhaps his most significant publication, however, was his 1952 book *Prehistoric Europe: The economic basis*, from which the following brief example of his writing is taken:

> If the comparatively minor role of sheep-breeding in the earliest husbandry of much of north-western Europe is to be associated with the general prevalence of forest at the time of the neolithic settlement, then it is only reasonable to suggest that its later rise to importance may have been due to a reduction in the extent of

woodland. That such must have occurred as an inevitable accompaniment of the progress of agriculture hardly needs emphasis. During the phase of shifting agriculture it is true that much clearance must have been of a transient character, the forest regenerating as the peasant farmers moved on to new lands, burning and felling as they went; yet, even at this stage, it is unlikely that regeneration was everywhere complete and it is known that on some of the poorer soils, such as those of central Jutland, stretches of heathland had come into being even at the time of the colonisation by battle-axe people. Progressively, under pressure of increasing density of settlement, the forest must have ceased to hold its own even on the richer soils and, within the area of primary settlement, permanently cleared zones must have increased in size. At the same time the system of shifting agriculture itself would gradually have broken down, leading by the end of the Bronze Age to the establishment of settled agriculture with fixed fields. (Clark 1952: 120)

Clark breathed new life into European prehistory; his ideas were innovative and his writing frequently had a clarity and readability that were attractive to readers. Anyone doubting that should read his 1939 book *Archaeology and society: Reconstructing the prehistoric past* (Clark 1957) and his 1940 book *Prehistoric England* (Clark 1944–1945), and then compare them with contemporary publications in the same field by other writers.

Stretching the literary boundaries

In the vanguard of the 'New Archaeologists' in the 1960s was Lewis R. Binford, an American archaeologist whose writings many readers found difficult to understand, but which others tried to imitate with disastrous results. John Cherry and Robin Torrence, who edited his 1983 book *In pursuit of the past: Decoding the archaeological record*, found it necessary in their editing 'to simplify as far as possible those passages made somewhat inaccessible by the famous Binford prose style' (Cherry and Torrence 1988: 10). Nevertheless, the writings of Binford and other New Archaeologists in America and Britain made important contributions to archaeological theory and method in the English-speaking world, although not on the European continent (Hodder 1991). For those readers who persevered, Binford's publications were not as abstruse as some claimed. The following passage is taken from his 1962 paper 'Archaeology as anthropology', published in the journal *American Antiquity*:

> Initially, it must be asked, "What are the aims of anthropology?" Most will agree that the integrated field is striving to *explicate* and *explain* the total range of physical and cultural similarities and differences characteristic of the entire spatial-temporal span of man's existence... Archaeology has certainly made major contributions as far as *explication* is concerned. Our current knowledge of the diversity which characterizes the range of extinct cultural systems is far superior to the limited knowledge available fifty years ago. Although this contribution is "admirable" and necessary, it has been noted that archaeology has made essentially no contribution in the realm of explanation...
>
> Before carrying this criticism further, some statement about what is meant by explanation must be offered. The meaning which explanation has within a scientific frame of reference is simply the *demonstration* of a constant articulation of variables within a system and the measurement of the concomitant variability among the variables within the system. Processual change in one variable can then be shown to relate in a predictable and quantifiable way to changes in other variables, the latter changing in turn relative to changes in the structure of the system as a whole. This approach to explanation presupposes concern with process, or the operation and structural modification of systems. It is suggested that archaeologists have not made major explanatory contributions to the field of anthropology because they do not conceive of archaeological data in a systemic frame of reference. Archaeological data are viewed particularistically and "explanation" is offered in terms of specific events rather than in terms of process... (Binford 1962: 217)

Such writing has set the tone for numerous archaeological theoreticians during the last few decades.

One of the more notable of these was British archaeologist David L. Clarke, a contemporary of mine at the University of Cambridge, with whom I collaborated on two early minor research projects (Clarke and Connah 1962; Connah 1962). Clarke died early in life but I remember him with some affection.

Each morning except Sunday he drank coffee with a group of us at the long-gone Hawkins' Café opposite Emmanuel College, and proved to be a most fluent conversationalist, particularly given to puns, which he rolled out effortlessly. However, he did not write nearly so well as he talked, as the following short passage from a paper in his 1972 edited book *Models in archaeology* demonstrates:

> Whilst it is likely that discarded artefacts and rubbish have suffered a "Brownian motion" of constant buffeting by animate and inanimate forces, nevertheless it is characteristic of Brownian motion in two dimensions that the buffeted particle will probably remain within a small radius of its point of deposition, given a long time span... Even where these continuous random walk processes were overridden by directed human activity, such as gathering and dumping rubbish, we may hypothesize that inertial tendencies would in most cases ensure that the majority of the rubbish collected would probably have been produced by the dumping group itself and gathered by them from the immediate vicinity of their focus of operations. (Clarke 1972a: 806)

A quotation taken out of context can be unfair to a writer, but in this case the reader might be justifiably mystified by 'Brownian motion' and by the complexity of the second sentence, of which an attempted translation follows:

> Even where chance was less important than human decisions, such as in collecting and throwing away rubbish, we may hypothesize that laziness would in most cases ensure that the people were mainly dumping their own rubbish and that they were gathering it from near where they lived.

I am uncertain of the accuracy of this translation. Does it really say what the writer wished to say? Perhaps not, but it is the primary duty of a writer to get his or her meaning over to the reader; if this is not done effectively then the reader should not carry all the blame for incomplete understanding.

Amongst the writers on archaeological theory in the late twentieth century was one with an unusual strategy for getting his message across. This was the American Kent V. Flannery, who at times used allegory, humour and satire to produce readable discussions written in the first person. As a consequence his writing was often both readily understood and enjoyable, particularly for those familiar with the contemporary archaeological literature. He liked to use dialogue, as in the following example:

> "Do you know Binford personally?" he finally asked.
>
> "Yes," I answered. "I was with him the day he fed 5000 undergraduates with a few loaves of bread and a newspaperful of fish". (Flannery 1976: 4)

An effective technique of Flannery's was the creation of fictional characters, who had a disturbing resemblance to different sorts of archaeologists familiar to many of us. Here is one of my favourite examples:

> The first guy, I suppose, came out of graduate school in the late 1960s, and he teaches now at a major department in the western United States. He began as a traditional archeologist, interested in Pueblo ruins and Southwestern prehistory, and he went on digs and surveys like the rest of us. Unlike the rest of us, he saw those digs and surveys not as an end in themselves, but as a means to an end, and a means that proved to be too slow. After a few years of dusty holes in hot, dreary valleys he was no closer to the top than when he had started, and in fact, he was showing signs of lamentable fallibility. In 50 tries at laying out a 5-ft square, he had never come closer than 4 ft 10 in by 5 ft 3 in, and he'd missed more floors than the elevator in the World Trade Center. And then, just when all seemed darkest, he discovered Philosophy of Science, and was born again.
>
> Suddenly he found the world would beat a path to his door if he criticized everyone else's epistemology. Suddenly he discovered that so long as his research design was superb, he never had to do the research; just publish the design, and it would be held up as a model, a brass ring hanging unattainable beyond the clumsy fingers of those who actually survey and dig. No more dust, no more heat, no more 5-ft squares. He worked in an office now, generating hypotheses and laws and models which an endless stream of graduate students was sent out to test; for he himself no longer did any fieldwork.
>
> And it was just as well, for as one of his former professors had said, "That poor wimp couldn't dig his way out of a kitty litter box." (Flannery 1982: 265–266)

Although Flannery's style was sometimes unusual, readers often remembered what he had written but forgot the often-laboured arguments of more 'scholarly' authors. His paper 'The golden Marshalltown: A parable for the archeology of the 1980s', from which came the last quotation, became a classic that is still admired by many readers.

In spite of the battles of the theoreticians, most archaeological writers of the last few decades continued to produce excavation reports, site surveys, artefact studies, methodological investigations, regional syntheses and all the rest of the gamut of publications, although often influenced by the new theoretical approaches. In addition, the last fifty years or so has seen an explosion in the production of university textbooks, to serve the growing number of archaeology students, as well as an increase in the number of 'popular' books and articles for an increasingly interested public. One of the most successful practitioners in both these media has been the British/American archaeologist Brian M. Fagan, whose best-known textbook, *People of the Earth: An introduction to world prehistory*, has gone through many editions. Writing textbooks makes very great demands on an author; they often cover enormous subject areas in a tightly controlled number of words, they must be as up to date as possible, they need to draw on an immense literature, their interpretations must be balanced, and on top of all of that they must be clearly written and easily read without trivializing the subject matter. Here is Fagan introducing the subject of urban origins, in the 1983 (fourth) edition of his *People of the Earth*:

> Archaeological research into early civilization concentrates on the origin and development of the city. Today the city is the primary human settlement type throughout the world, and it has become so since the Industrial Revolution altered the economic face of the globe. The earliest cities assumed many forms, from the compact, walled settlement of Mesopotamia to the Mesoamerican ceremonial center with a core population in its precincts and a scattered rural population in villages arranged over the surrounding landscape. The cities of the Harappan civilization of the Indus were carefully planned communities with regular streets and assigned quarters for different living groups. The palaces of the Minoans and Mycenaeans functioned as secular economic and trading centers that served as a focus for scattered village populations nearby.

> A city is best defined by its population, which is generally larger
> and denser than that of towns or villages. As we have said, a good
> and generally used rule of thumb is a lower limit of 5000 people
> for a city. However, numbers are not a sufficient determinant:
> Many people can congregate in a limited area and still not possess
> the compact diversity of population which enables the economic
> and organizational complexity of a city to develop. It is this com-
> plexity that distinguishes the city from other settlement types.
> Most cities have a complexity in both organization and nonagri-
> cultural activities which is supported by large food surpluses. The
> city is not merely complex; it is a functioning part of a complex
> system of different settlements which rely on its many services
> and facilities. (Fagan 1983: 265–266)

The writing of textbooks and books for a general readership has
often been regarded by more pedantic academic archaeologists
as an activity of marginal importance and one that does not
require 'real' research. In fact nothing could be further from
the truth, and anyone who writes about archaeology can learn
something about archaeological writing by reading a selection of
such publications.

Meanwhile, other writers have tackled increasingly difficult
subject matter, as post-processual archaeology, symbolic archaeology, cognitive archaeology or other new approaches to the
data have influenced their ways of thinking. One such author is
Anne Elizabeth Yentsch, an American archaeologist whose 1994
book *A Chesapeake family and their slaves: A study in historical
archaeology* has made an important contribution to the relatively
new subject of historical archaeology. In a foreword to her book,
James Deetz describes it as 'a study in historical ethnography or
anthropological history' (Deetz in Yentsch 1994: xix). Certainly,
it is far less concerned with the details of archaeological data than
many writers have been in the past. Here is a brief sample:

> It is hard to know to what extent Benedict Calvert was con-
> sciously aware of the symbolic structure that he was alter-
> ing; his evaluation may well have been cast in terms of what
> seemed appropriate and what seemed out-of-date. The fashion-
> able changes made to the house, and in particular its front fore-
> court, also presented Maryland natives with an opportunity for
> symbolic inversion. This provides a more vivid example of the

way Annapolitans consciously knew of and used the visual symbols that dominated their cultural landscape. It occurred with the construction of the large, ornate, octagonal privy beside the State House in the 1780s... While the replication of style may have been a political act of appropriation (symbolically inverting the prior order), or the emulation and use of a newly fashionable form, in terms of the positional relationships it set up on the State Circle landscape, an opposition between the octagonal forecourt at the Calvert house and the outhouse was clearly set in place. And shortly thereafter, the octagonal forecourt at the Calvert site was removed. (Yentsch 1994: 274–275)

Such imaginative writing is merely part of an increasingly diverse treatment of archaeology by its authors. In recent years there has been a tidal wave of books and papers, many of them by writers questioning previous interpretations and seeking new perspectives. One such author is British archaeologist Peter Mitchell, whose 2005 book, *African connections: An archaeological perspective on Africa and the wider world*, is an innovative addition to studies of the African past. Here is part of the beginning of Chapter 1:

> This chapter provides the background for the rest of the book. The first question considered is, What is Africa? To answer this I look at the term's origins and how it has come to be applied to the entirety of the continent. Next I examine the degree to which Africa can be considered to be a coherent whole and how far the frequent separation of sub-Saharan Africa from the rest of the continent is warranted. Attention then turns to the continent's physical geography and how its climate, physiography, and ecology constitute the frontiers through which African populations have interacted with each other and the wider world. These interfaces have been, and continue to be, framed by what Africa produces and what its inhabitants have sought from abroad, as well as by the organizational and logistical structures through which these resources were exploited and moved. Discussion of the material, social, and technological bases of Africa's connections with the rest of the world forms the third part of this chapter.

> From here I move to how archaeologists have thought about these connections. Early speculations that emphasized the passive receipt of external influences were closely linked to European

colonial conceptualizations of Africa as a "dark" and "timeless" continent where little changed except through contact from outside. Such ideas, which long influenced Africanist scholarship, still cast a shadow today. (Mitchell 2005: 1–2)

Archaeological writing in recent times has also become increasingly technical, as some authors coped with an expanding range of 'scientific' data. Chemical analyses, metallurgy, archaeobotany, archaeozoology, magnetics, genetics, linguistics, complex dating methods, sophisticated statistics: the list is almost endless. Without doubt, subjects of this sort present the author or authors (because this sort of writing is often multi-authored) with special problems. Inevitably, much of what they write will be intended for readers belonging to the specialized subject area in which they work, but it will often need to be comprehensible also to a wider archaeological readership and at times even to readers outside the discipline. Consequently, carefully structured prose, clearly expressed, should be the goal, but unfortunately this is not always attained. In addition, the level of explanation will need to be appropriate for the targeted readership. Here is a good example of such writing, taken from a journal paper about human parasite eggs from seventeenth to nineteenth-century privies in Albany, New York:

> The population density within Albany and the absence of both a supply of clean water and a sanitary system of waste removal are largely responsible for the poor health conditions found in this urban environment. The cultural resource studies cited here have archaeologically documented the rise of parasite infections among the residents of Albany during the 17th and 18th centuries. The description of the parasites and their respective life cycles creates a new perspective on the historical living conditions in this city. Five different human parasites were identified in the archaeological samples collected from Albany. They include the *Ascaris* (roundworm), *Trichuris* (whipworm), *Taenia* (tapeworm), *Hymenolepiasis nana* (dwarf tapeworm), and the first archaeological observation of the parasite *Macracanthorhynchus hirudinaceus* (thorny-headed worm). Other eggs were observed as oval, transparent, and embryonate eggs that contained a small worm that could be from a number of species. These eggs were classified as strongylates.

A roundworm of dogs, *Toxocara canis*, was discovered from 40 Howard Street during the period the city market was located here, before the residential development of the lots. Eggs of this parasite can be passed from dogs to humans. In addition to these parasites, analysis of sediment samples from the Picotte-DEC site revealed evidence of pinworm (*Enterobius vermicularis*) and louse nits (*Pediculus humanus*). The presence of lice is relevant to the health conditions in the city because they can transmit typhus. (Fisher et al. 2007: 187)

By this stage the average reader might well be feeling distinctly uncomfortable. One does not have to be an invertebrate zoologist to get the message from this account: in some places the 'good old days' were not so good after all!

Conclusion

The twenty-five writers that have been discussed in this chapter are a personal, perhaps idiosyncratic, selection that fails to include many others who have made notable contributions to archaeological publication. However, the intention has been to sample the enormous archaeological literature in English from the sixteenth century to the beginning of the twenty-first century, in order to gain an impression of archaeological writing over that long period. Readers dissatisfied with my choices are welcome to make their own selection. The point is that we should make ourselves aware of what has gone before, and not merely write in an historical vacuum. Reflecting on the writings that have been considered, it is apparent that there has been a wide range of subject matter that has been treated in a variety of ways, depending on the knowledge and ideas of the time and on the intended audience. There have also been marked differences in prose style and in writing skills, although these should be judged by the standards and fashions of the relevant time. To review the history of archaeological writing inevitably draws attention to the history of archaeology itself. The authors who have been sampled reveal an early emphasis on technology and chronology, which has gradually been replaced by a range of broader interests including economy, ecology, social organization, ideology, symbolism and other aspects of the past. Indeed the history of archaeological writing is one of an expanding recognition of what constitutes archaeological evidence and how information about past peoples can be wrung from it. Changing perceptions of the past have also shaped archaeological writing. What we write at present will merely be another stage in the shifting images that result, and it is hoped that we will not persuade ourselves that ours is the ultimate interpretation.

Three

Readership determines form

For whom are we writing?

When beginning to write, the first thing to decide is who are to be the readers of what we are about to write. It is most unlikely that a satisfactory dialogue can be developed between author and readers unless the latter have been correctly identified from the very beginning. As Matthews, Bowen and Matthews (2000: 99) perceptively remark, 'The essential difficulty [in writing] is in trying to ensure that the thoughts created in the mind of the reader are the same thoughts that were in your mind'. Consequently, the writer must shape what is written to suit the intended audience. Most obviously, this means there will be considerable variation in technical and theoretical content and attendant explanation: specialists in the writer's field will want the details of the basic data but will not need their context explained; in contrast nonspecialists will need to know what the data mean but will not want their minutiae. Similarly, the structure of a piece of writing – its paragraph and sentence forms, its prose style, its use of metaphor, its choice of words, its type of illustrations and tables and so on – should be varied to suit the potential readers. In particular, as archaeological writers, we must try to avoid what some have perceived as a problem in social and cultural anthropological writing, which has been accused by one of its own profession of 'hibernating in a difficult language' (Eriksen 2005: 1). In the end, a writer's task is to communicate with the reader at the selected level of comprehension. If the reader fails to understand, or finds it necessary to read a sentence several times over, she or he is not necessarily stupid as some writers might claim; it could be that the writer has not written at the appropriate level. All of this is easier to say than to do. In my own writing I have often tried to imagine myself as one of the intended readers, and have asked myself whether as that person I would understand what has been written. The problem is that it is too easy to convince oneself that all is well, and this is where one must seek the opinion of others, particularly those who might become part of the intended readership. This is discussed later in this book, but suffice it to say that in my own case I have sometimes so misjudged the potential readership that my writing has been more successful with readers for whom it was not actually intended.

The identity of the intended readership will also influence the choice of publication outlet, although in practice it will often be the other way round, so that a prospective outlet will predetermine the readership. In any event, it is the readership that will shape the form of what is written. Hard economic reality plays an important part in this; how many readers are there likely to be and how much will they, or the libraries that serve them, be prepared to pay to read your work? An author is entitled to have ideals about the nature of a particular archaeological publication but also needs to accept that the cost of publication will weigh heavily on what is written and how it is done. Circumstances can be very different for a commercial publisher who risks money in the hope of profitable sales, for a subsidized academic or institutional publisher who at best might break even from a much more limited market and for a society or journal that is financed only by subscribers and will sell mainly to libraries and specialists. Within these generalized categories of publishers there are numerous variations, and there is also the practice of private publication either on paper or on the Internet. The important point is that it is wise for the intending author to think about how publication is to be achieved *before* commencing to write.

Inevitably, these matters create a tension between what an author wishes to write and what a publisher or an editor is prepared to accept for publication. Frequently this tension concerns the length of a piece of writing, with less experienced authors often finding it difficult to work within the constraints imposed upon them by the character of the chosen publication outlet. For instance, although it is difficult to generalize, many publishers will want to limit the length of a book to 100,000 words, and although there are exceptions, journal editors are often unhappy about papers longer than 5,000 words. Problems of length can become particularly severe if an author either decides or is obliged to change the publication outlet after the writing has already been completed. An author is wise to keep a very close watch on the number of words as the writing actually proceeds, a task that is now very much easier to do accurately than before word processors were available. Detailed and sometimes drastic pruning at the revision stage, which is discussed later in this book, will also often be necessary if an author is to be spared criticism for verbosity by publishers' readers or editors' referees. In addition, there is always the risk of outright rejection by a publisher or editor because of excessive length or the risk of having to rewrite in order to reduce the length.

Another common cause of tension between author and publication outlet is one that characterizes any writing that relies heavily on illustrations, as is the case with most archaeological writing. The type and number of illustrations have long been matters of contention, with authors' expectations often exceeding what publishers and editors are willing to accept. This was particularly the case in the old days of acid-etched line blocks and half-tone photographs that had to be printed on glossy paper, the latter requiring separate pages known as 'tip-ins' to be inserted into the printed text. I can recollect many an argument with editor or publisher about the number of illustrations that I could include in a paper or book; because photographs were more expensive to reproduce than line drawings they were usually the principal cause of disagreement. As for photographs in colour, they were almost always out of the question, so that even coloured glass beads, for instance, had to be illustrated uselessly in black and white. Fortunately times have changed; in the last few decades there has been a revolution in printing technology, so that both drawings and photographs can now be printed on the same paper as the text (even if sometimes done rather badly) and even colour illustration is increasingly common. Furthermore, illustrations can be submitted in a digital form for publication, although technical problems can sometimes make hard copy preferable. Nevertheless, illustrations still complicate publication and increase its cost, albeit less than formerly. As a result, archaeological authors are still told how many and what sort of illustrations they can include in their work, and this nearly always limits what they would really like to have.

Archaeological publication has a variety of forms, which can be roughly divided into three main groups. First, there are monographs; that is to say, single- or multiple-authored books or edited collections of papers by different authors. Second, there are journals (also called serials or periodicals) of which separate issues appear usually at regular intervals and that are often edited by members of the archaeological profession acting in an honorary capacity. Third, there are miscellaneous publications that can range very widely in content and readership, everything from general interest popular magazines, to newspapers, to guidebooks; indeed, a great variety of outlets. Perhaps the large number of archaeological consultants' reports should also be included in this group, but some would argue that they do not constitute publication because of their typically limited circulation. In recognizing these three basic groups, it should also be added that archaeologists might sometimes find themselves writing for television or for video or film, all of these constituting other distinct forms of publication, although here included in the miscellaneous category. Furthermore, increasingly the distinction between publication in print and publication online will influence the form that archaeological writing takes. Quite apart from many books and journals now being available on the Internet as well as in a printed form, there is also the growth of publication in a digital form only, what has become known as 'born digital' (Harvey 2005: 14). Thus the British journal *Internet Archaeology* has been published since 1996 and produces articles that 'make use of the huge potential of Internet publication to present archaeological research in unique and exciting ways, such as full colour images, photographs, searchable data sets, visualisations and interactive mapping' (*Internet Archaeology* home page). It is tempting to think that this represents the future of archaeological publishing, but as discussed in Chapter 1, uncertainty about long-term digital archiving remains a matter of concern. It could be that such material eventually proves to have been ephemeral.

Archaeological monographs

The most substantial form of archaeological publication is still the printed monograph, but it can appear in many shapes and sizes. Perhaps pre-eminent is the monographic research study, often a report on one or more excavations or other fieldwork or an investigation of a class of artefacts, and frequently incorporating sections written by other specialists. In the later nineteenth century and through most of the twentieth century, publications of this sort formed the backbone of archaeological publication and in some instances assumed an almost iconic status. Pitt Rivers and Wheeler, already mentioned in Chapter 2, produced model publications of this sort, heavily descriptive and loaded with detailed information as well as being comprehensively illustrated. Petrie did much the same for Ancient Egypt, and in the Americas and many other parts of the world such publications also appeared. So massively detailed were many of them that they themselves constitute a data set susceptible to further research. Thus in 1972 David Clarke was able to reanalyse the evidence from a prehistoric settlement at Glastonbury, in Somerset, England, that had been excavated between 1892 and 1907 and published in two substantial and exemplary volumes in 1911 and 1917 (Bulleid and Gray 1911, 1917; Clarke 1972a). However, the preparation of such a monograph could be a massive undertaking, making very heavy demands on time and finances, in order to produce a publication whose subject matter and cost resulted in only limited sales. Not surprisingly some intended volumes never appeared or did so only after a delay of many years. Perhaps the most remarkable example of this was the publication of John Garstang's excavations at Meroë, in the Sudan, eighty-three years after their completion (Török 1997).

Monographic research studies still appear from time to time but commercial publishers are wary of taking them on without a substantial subsidy, and publication usually becomes the task of research institutions, like the British Institute in Eastern Africa that has produced a string of research memoirs over the last four decades. In addition, generous universities like that at Uppsala in Sweden regularly publish archaeological postgraduate theses. There are also the remarkable British Archaeological Reports, handled by a consortium of Oxford publishers who have produced well over 1,000 archaeological monographs in the last thirty-odd years, featuring research from just about anywhere in the world that in many cases would not otherwise have been published. Furthermore, the United States is especially fortunate in the number of universities and other institutions that have been willing to publish specialist monographs. Harvard University's massive *Excavations at Seibal* (Willey 1988) is a good example, but the University of California and the Wenner-Gren Foundation and others have also made remarkable contributions. Nevertheless, the archaeological author who sets out to write a research monograph is courageous. It can take a very long time (sometimes measured in years) and create such a gap in an archaeologist's publications that research-grant committees and appointments boards begin to suspect inactivity. Younger archaeological authors should beware and should note that some highly successful archaeologists have never written a research monograph in their lives!

A more common form of archaeological monograph and one that is usually more commercially viable is the scholarly synthesis. Frequently its subject matter consists of a review of current knowledge concerning some discrete area of the archaeological discipline. It might for instance be a regional study, or a chronologically ordered analysis of a particular period in the past or a combination of both approaches. Alternatively it might be a guide to some aspect of archaeological methodology or a discussion of archaeological theory. In some cases it might even break away from generally accepted interpretations and attempt an innovative examination of some part of the discipline. Indeed, such books can range very widely across the multifaceted subject of archaeology, and all of us can think of numerous examples of publications of this sort. They are usually intended for archaeologically knowledgeable readers, such as members of the profession or university students, both undergraduate and post-graduate. Some books of this type might also attempt to reach the general reading public, but this can be difficult to accomplish. Commonly they are published by commercial publishers who have access to international markets, but universities and other scholarly institutions and societies also produce such material, although their distribution potential is often more limited. Many archaeologists will write monographic syntheses in the course of their careers, either as sole authors or in collaboration, and there has been an explosion of this sort of publication over the last half-century. Acquiring and marshalling data for such books can be difficult and time consuming, and the actual writing time can vary enormously from a few months to several years. It is also essential to provide books of this sort with a detailed list of references and in-text referencing. In some cases they might in addition require footnotes or endnotes and appendices. Nevertheless, synthesis writing is a challenging task that any aspiring archaeologist can attempt and one that potentially can make a real contribution to the discipline. This is particularly the case if the intending writer is not in too much of a hurry. A surprising number of archaeological syntheses in recent years have quickly faded from view because of their superficial, often hastily written and sometimes inaccurate content. Publication runs are often short, sales indifferent, and discounting as remainders all too frequent. Admittedly this can be the fate of good books as well as weaker ones, but it is important to take one's time and do the very best job that one can.

As already indicated, the readers of general syntheses will inevitably include many who are studying archaeology or related disciplines at universities. However, there is also the distinct genre of monograph known as the 'textbook'. This is a highly specialized area of writing, publishing and marketing. Brian Fagan, who has been one of the most successful authors of archaeological textbooks in recent times, has rightly claimed that writing books of this sort 'means joining a different world' (Fagan 2006a: 48). Textbooks are most commonly written for undergraduate readers by university academics with experience of teaching at that level. In practice many of them probably originate from actual courses that their authors have taught. The resulting texts tend to be structured in a somewhat mechanical fashion, with complex hierarchies of headings and subheadings, heavy use of bold or italic type, 'boxes' that examine in more detail aspects of the subject dealt with more generally in the main text, numerous illustrations including coloured ones and glossaries of specialized terms. In addition, such books are sometimes supplied with introductory advice for the 'instructor', revision questions at the end of chapters or of the whole book and even links to associated Web sites. These are some of the proliferating strategies that have become an obligatory part of the intellectual spoon-feeding that now characterizes university education in much of the Western world. The archaeologist who writes such material will need to develop a special expertise and should be aware of the danger that colleagues will dismiss such publications as not constituting 'real research' and therefore as academically inferior. It is particularly necessary to be cautious before agreeing to write for one of the multi-authored mega-textbooks that are sometimes commissioned. By the time you have revised your chapter several times to fit in with the other two dozen or so contributors, pleased the general editor and added and subtracted bits to pacify a publisher who is more concerned about marketability than about your interpretation of the past, you will finish up with dull, anaemic writing that you wish you had never put your name to. Nevertheless, there is an almost insatiable market for archaeological textbooks, and it is important that they be written by scholars as well as by specialist educators. Perhaps all academic archaeologists should at least consider attempting one such book or book chapter in the course of their careers.

Another form of monograph that has become increasingly common in recent times is the edited collection of commissioned papers, sometimes emanating from a conference; however, it is different from most traditional conference proceedings discussed later in that the papers invariably have a common unifying theme and are properly refereed. Many archaeologists have written for volumes of this type at one time or another, and some have become more noted for their editing of such publications than for their own writing. It is a characteristic of these books that they attempt to provide the latest 'state of the art' information on various aspects of the selected topic, and therefore publication attempts to be speedy and slower writers can find themselves excluded at the last minute. Monographs of this sort make important contributions to the discipline, although they sometimes quickly go out of date. Contributors find that writing for them is rather like writing a journal paper (discussed later), but there has to be an adherence to the general theme of the work, a constraint that will vary depending on the focus and determination of the editor or editors. The published product can range from a tightly coherent work to a loose agglomeration in which some papers are of doubtful relevance. Before writing for a 'collected' volume, the prospective author should not be blinded by the invitation to contribute, but should carefully assess the prospects of successful publication. Inevitably there have been cases where archaeological authors have written tailor-made papers for publications that never eventuated.

There is a similar if not greater danger in the case of another type of monograph that has been around for many years but from time to time seems to be in its death throes. This is the dedicated conference volume or 'proceedings', usually identified by the name, place and date of the conference at which its constituent papers were presented. Because these proceedings are often bulky and expensive to produce, there is perhaps no better way of really frightening publishers than by suggesting they publish such a volume. Frequently lacking coherence of content, with editors who have done little to ensure a quality product, and often consisting of papers that have not been refereed, conference proceedings usually have limited sales. Furthermore, the publication by participating authors of the same material elsewhere, most commonly in a journal, frequently overtakes the often-interim contributions to the discipline made by conference proceedings. This is just as well because such proceedings can take years to appear or never appear at all. A particularly remarkable example of both delay and publication failure is provided by the PanAfrican Association for Prehistory and Related Studies (the name has varied over the years). In contrast to the speedy 1996 publication of the proceedings of its 1995 conference in Harare, Zimbabwe (Pwiti and Soper 1996), the proceedings of its 1983 conference in Jos, Nigeria (Andah, de Maret and Soper 1993), took ten years to appear! More recently, the proceedings of the 2005 conference in Gaborone, Botswana, seems to have died completely. In short, the archaeological author should be careful about contributing to such publications; particularly writers in the earlier part of their careers cannot afford to have their work delayed for years or possibly never produced at all.

There is also the specialized collection of edited papers known as the 'Festschrift', a German word that has been imported into English to describe a collection of writings published in honour of a particularly distinguished scholar. This sort of monograph is usually composed of papers by former students or colleagues of the individual to whom it is dedicated. Often its creation remains unknown to the recipient of this honour until it is presented to her or him on the occasion of retirement or a birthday late in life. It is one of the kinder practices in the sometimes cheerless world of scholarly competition. To be asked by its editor or editors to contribute to such a volume is itself something of an honour and one that can be difficult to decline. However, the archaeological author would be wise to accept that the resulting book will most likely be an example of the 'curate's egg', good in parts and therefore by inference not good in others. Some contributors will have written papers of importance, others will have produced ones at best described as inconsequential, and still others will have dusted off typescripts that they had lying around and had been unsure what to do with. Consequently, the publication of a Festschrift can often be quickly forgotten, and sad to say, some can sink without trace. This is also because typically they are badly distributed. Some years ago I contributed a paper to a Festschrift for a retired professor from the Sorbonne, but because of a variety of circumstances some twenty years went by before I even saw a copy of the published result (Connah 1981b). Indeed, there is a greater chance of a Festschrift being remembered if it takes the form of a dedicated volume of an established journal (e.g., Smith et al. 2004), a strategy that is sometimes adopted because of the difficulty of financing the publication of a special volume.

In contrast to essentially specialist books like the last six types, there are also books written for the 'general reader', whatever that might mean. These are what Brian Fagan has accurately called 'trade books' (Fagan 2006a: 48). They can take a bewildering variety of forms, everything from the glossy highly illustrated 'coffee-table' book to the humble paperback. A major consideration is that they must be saleable, preferably in large numbers, and their success will depend as much on a commercial publisher's marketing strategies as on their quality. Essentially, an author writing this sort of monograph must assume that readers will have little or no specialized knowledge, but must be careful not to patronize them nor to 'dumb down' the book's content. Nevertheless, it will be necessary to explain matters that a professional readership would take for granted, and the writer will need to simplify the more technical material, compress the more detailed data and shorten alternative interpretations of evidence. In addition, in such publications it is usual to limit the referencing, or reduce it to a list of 'further reading' or even omit it altogether, in order to improve readability. Above all, 'popular' books of this type must be interesting to read, a characteristic that can be difficult to achieve unless the writer is genuinely enthusiastic about the subject and has considerable literary skills. Far from being a form of writing that in the opinion of some archaeologists is beneath their notice, these publications can play an important part in establishing people's awareness of their own heritage. In many areas of the world where the documentary record is limited or absent, books of this sort are particularly needed, but are still not getting the attention from writers that they deserve.

Archaeological journals

The second main form of archaeological publication consists of journals or, as they are often called, serials or periodicals. As the latter names indicate, these are essentially publications that are supposed to appear at regular intervals, although their performance in this respect is sometimes unsatisfactory. Each issue has a volume number and sometimes a part number, as well as a date, and some older journals have been known to add to the prospective reader's problems by inserting the words 'New Series' and starting their numbering all over again. Occasionally, they go one better and change the actual title of the journal, and might even do this more than once. Fifty years ago, when I was a student of archaeology, there were far fewer archaeological monographs for us to read than is now the case; as a result we relied heavily on journal papers and came to regard such publications as the *Proceedings of the Prehistoric Society* or *Antiquity* or *American Antiquity* as old friends. We also learned to appreciate that although all monographs by their very nature were out of date, recent journal papers had a greater chance of presenting new evidence and current thinking. This, indeed, remains the principal attraction of journal publication for the archaeological author. It provides the opportunity to make new research or interpretations available quickly, thus not only advancing the discipline but also staking the author's claim as the originator of the relevant material. That, at least, is theoretically the case, even though in practice some journals move at a snail's pace.

Journals tend to be devoted to specific areas, periods or aspects of archaeological scholarship, although some have broader interests and will publish papers ranging widely across the discipline. Because such publications act as vehicles for the rapid dissemination of information, all professional archaeologists will write for journals at some stage during their careers and some will produce papers counted in the hundreds. Indeed, an archaeologist's earliest experience of writing for publication is likely to be in this form. One of the first lessons to learn, therefore, is how to choose the most suitable journal for a particular paper. There are perhaps four major considerations in making this choice. The first is to select a journal whose focus includes the subject of your paper, but this choice is not always as easy as it might seem. I remember once sending a paper to an anthropological journal that returned it with the comment that it was not anthropological enough, so I sent it to an archaeological journal that returned it with the comment that it was not archaeological enough. Subsequently, I published it in a journal devoted to the geographical area with which the paper was concerned. Undoubtedly, the mistake had been my own, not that of the respective journal editors. The second consideration in selecting a journal is the time that publication might take. Some journals appear only once a year, others several times a year. Some are very selective, have a high rejection rate and will fast-track papers that are judged important; others accept most of the material that they are sent and have a serious backlog that might delay the publication of your paper several years. In addition, journals vary in the expedition with which they handle the refereeing and revision process, and it has now become common for journal papers to state their submission date, revision date and acceptance date on their first page, so that the reader can assess how up to date they are. Therefore, before choosing a journal it is a good idea to look at some of its recent volumes to see how long the publication process has been taking. The third thing to take into account when choosing a journal is the length and relevance of the paper that you wish to submit. There is no point in sending an 8,000-word paper to a journal that stipulates that papers should not exceed 5,000 words in length. There is also a lot of difference between a journal devoted to brief reports about the latest research and one that is prepared to publish detailed site, excavation or artefact studies. The fourth matter to consider in choosing a journal is its format and production quality. Archaeological papers in which illustrations and tables have an important role are best published in a large-format journal, not a small one. Some archaeological journals are too small to be useful vehicles for publication, except perhaps for theoretical or synthetic writing. The quality of printing, particularly of illustrations, is also important in deciding on a journal; some current journals leave a lot to be desired in this respect. You do not want drawings on which you have expended many hours of work, for instance, to appear as if an ink-soaked frog has hopped across the page.

Just as with monographs, journals also vary greatly in their degree of specialization. For instance, there is a world of difference between a research-oriented publication like *Archaeometry* and one intended for the general reader like *Current Archaeology*, which is aimed at the 'middle market' and with a circulation of 18,000 claims to be 'Britain's leading archaeological magazine' (*Current Archaeology* 2008). Clearly, archaeologists have to suit the content and presentation of their paper to the policy of those who fund and those who edit the journal for which they are writing. However, editors sometimes find that prospective authors give insufficient attention to suiting their writing to the level of readership for which the journal is intended. In contrast, there are writers who are so aware of this problem that they will publish the same material at two levels in order to reach both a specialized readership and the interested public. For example, Peter Robertshaw wrote about phytolith evidence for what could be Africa's earliest bananas in both the presti-gious *Journal of Archaeological Science*, where he collaborated with two other authors (Lejju, Robertshaw and Taylor 2006), and on his own in the popular American magazine *Archaeology* (Robertshaw 2006). Given the considerable growth of public interest in archaeology throughout much of the Western world in recent years, the archaeological author will find an increasing demand for periodical writing at a popular level.

This raises the question of another distinction amongst jour-nals that is important: their division into those that are refereed and those that are not. Modern pressures on academic archaeol-ogists to publish only in the most reputable journals have placed great emphasis on the refereeing process. Some archaeologists are even of the opinion that writing for any nonrefereed outlet is a waste of time, although this is an extreme view. For exam-ple, 'newsletters', as they are frequently called, are usually not refereed, but they have an important role to play in rapidly dis-seminating information. They are often the quickest means of doing this, particularly as many of them are now available on the Internet, sometimes without any printed equivalent. Jour-nals intended for a nonprofessional readership will also tend to publish articles that have not been formally refereed, but in most cases writers will find that satisfying the requirements of editorial staff can be an almost equivalent challenge. Clearly, the archaeo-logical writer must be careful regarding nonrefereed publication, but properly used it still does have a role.

Many journals also publish another form of writing that is not refereed, although editorial interference with submitted material is not unknown. This is the book review or, less commonly, the review article about a recently published book. Writing of this sort is an important means of making readers aware of the lat-est published monographs and providing guidance concerning their content and quality. However, a review writer might on occasion be so unimpressed by a book that the resulting review is severely critical, perhaps even including remarks verging on libel or slander. Unless such comments can be proved to be false or malicious, legal action by the author of the book might be unlikely, but professional relationships can be seriously strained by insensitive remarks and it is wise to avoid them. In any case, book-review editors, who are often different from the main editor or editors of a journal, might ask for the review to be 'toned down'. Policies on this matter vary from journal to journal, some editors being prepared to stimulate controversy, whereas others are so careful that their published reviews become anodyne and of limited value for the purpose that they are meant to serve. However, the main question for the archaeological author is whether the writing of book reviews is a worthwhile activity. In the opinion of some people, book reviews do not constitute publications that can be listed on one's personal bibliography, and therefore writing them is a waste of time. In contrast, others insist that writing reviews is worthwhile because it provides them with free copies of books that they could otherwise not afford to purchase. This latter view is one that I have my doubts about. Although there are some dishonest review writers who do not read the book in question with sufficient care, for those who do read it thoroughly there is a price to pay in the number of days that might have been devoted to other work. Furthermore, authors of archaeological books sometimes complain about people who write book reviews who have never written a book themselves. Nevertheless, book reviews have an important role to play, and archaeological authors will inevitably be affected by them, either as commentaries on their own work or as a means of commenting on the work of others.

Miscellaneous publications

The third main form of archaeological publication is the miscellaneous category. This includes nonarchaeological popular magazines, newspapers, guidebooks, travel literature, encyclopaedias, exhibition catalogues and many other outlets – to which might be added other distinct forms of publication such as television, film, video and the Internet. In particular, writing for the visual media will probably become increasingly important in the future and, as some archaeologists have already found, at times sufficiently lucrative to be attractive. It is also the case that producing smaller pieces for a variety of general publications is a good way to develop one's writing skills, particularly with respect to matching content and style to readership. Archaeologists solely concerned with more scholarly writing might question this idea, but as stressed in the first chapter of this book, the problem with archaeological writing is that it is not enough to know one's archaeology; one must also know how to write. The best way to do this is to do it; practice at every and any level can be worthwhile.

Conclusion

There is a great variety of writing in which an archaeological author can become engaged. The categories that have been discussed range widely and often have only vaguely defined boundaries. For example, there exists a type of monograph that is published as part of a numbered series over a period of years and yet it is not technically a journal. Thus the publication *Archaeological method and theory* ran to eleven volumes. Librarians regard such publications as a sort of bibliographical grey area that creates cataloguing problems, and as a result library users can sometimes find them difficult to locate. Nevertheless, in spite of the great diversity of archaeological writing, one matter remains constant. This is that the character of the readership for which it is intended determines the individual form of a piece of writing. Therefore, the first question that we must always ask ourselves is, Whom are we writing for? Unless we can answer this question before we even start to write, there is a danger that there will be few readers of what we have written. If that happens, we will probably have wasted our time writing.

Four

Turning data into text

Images of the past

More than sixty years ago I came upon some illustrations in a book at primary school that made a lasting impression on me. They were black-and-white drawings of what was then known as Glastonbury Lake-Village, in Somerset, England, showing how it had looked in the late first millennium BC when it was occupied. Already referred to in Chapter 3, this site had been the subject of a model excavation for its time at the turn of the nineteenth and twentieth centuries, its results published in exemplary fashion in two large volumes (Bulleid and Gray 1911, 1917). The illustrations that so caught my childish imagination were by the artist Amédée Forestier (Phillips 2005), one showing a bird's-eye view of the village and the other showing villagers on its landing stage and in canoes adjacent to it. These pictures were originally published, together with other illustrations of the village, in the *Illustrated London News* on 2 December 1911 (*Illustrated London News* 1911: 928–933). At present, my easiest access to copies of these illustrations is in a small introductory text entitled *The lake-villages of Somerset* (Bulleid 1958), where each is captioned 'supposititious', a rather ugly word meaning 'spurious' or 'substituted for the real' (Allen 1990). Indeed, although based on excavated evidence, the Forestier drawings might be far removed from the reality of two thousand years ago, resulting as they do from the imagination of an early-twentieth-century artist, who had been born in Paris in 1854. Nevertheless, they serve as a reminder of the basic task for archaeological authors, that of imagining the past, of forming a mental image of a past that is dead and can only be resurrected in terms of our own interpretation of the evidence available to us. As Carmel Schrire has written, 'Only imagination fleshes out the sound and taste of time past, anchoring the flavor of lost moments in the welter of objects left behind' (Schrire 1995: 11). For some periods documents might assist in this enterprise, but even then our picture of the past will be partly a product of our mental processes that have selected and interpreted the relevant information. This problem is reflected in the introspection about archaeological writing that has occupied some archaeologists (e.g., Writing archaeology 1989; Gosden 1992).

The writer shapes the past

As shown in Chapters 2 and 3, archaeological writing can take many forms, so many that generalizing about the subject might seem impossible. However, whether writing is about primary data, synthetic interpretation, methodology, theory or other matters, everything that is written is shaped by the writer's perceptions, cultural context, education and experience, as well as by the relevant data and the writer's knowledge of archaeology. E. H. Carr's aphorism – 'Before you study the history, study the historian' (Carr 1961: 38) – applies also to archaeology: before you study the archaeology, study the archaeologist. It is doubtful if archaeological writing can ever be as objective as was formerly often claimed. The archaeological author must try to be aware of the influences that inevitably shape what is written and how it is written. It is necessary to accept that there can hardly be such a thing as an atheoretical approach. Even those of us who might claim to have no interest in archaeological theory are affected by it, often I suspect without being conscious of the particular theory unwittingly promoted. Archaeological theorists seem to expect writers to be explicit about their theoretical stance and to make this quite clear to their readers, but this is sometimes not easy to do because of uncertainty about theory by the writers themselves. There are also those writers who incline towards a medley of archaeological theory, although some might regard this as merely the consequence of muddled thinking.

Whatever the case, it is important that a writer does ask herself or himself some hard questions about theoretical issues before commencing to write. Whether or not it is appropriate to identify with a particular theoretical orientation, such as processualism, post-processualism, Marxism or agency theory, the writer should try to help the reader to understand the way in which the past and its material evidence have been interpreted. Because archaeological writers create imagined pasts as they try to make human history out of things and their contexts, it is important that the reader be made aware of what has shaped their imagining. As for those who write about archaeological theory itself, they will have a particularly difficult task if they are to get their message across even to a professional readership; presenting complex arguments with clarity and precision and explaining esoteric concepts and specialized language can be very difficult. Perhaps the most effective way of doing this is by means of appropriate case studies, which show how particular theories can be applied to the archaeological data. Thus the theorists need not only to explain what they think we should be doing; they also need to show us how to do it.

However, in practice archaeological theory is far too important to leave to the archaeological theorists alone. As has been claimed, 'Since the late 1950s the discipline has been rent by endless academic disputes about the ways we should think about the past and its material remains, and how to make deeper sense of earlier societies' (Bintliff 2008: 147). There has been an increasing awareness by archaeologists of the circumstantial and often intractable nature of the evidence that forms their basic raw material, as well as a broadening appreciation of what constitutes such evidence. Historians have a difficult enough job interpreting the documents available to them, even though people who lived at the time being investigated wrote many of them and have thus provided direct contact with the past. Archaeologists face a greater level of uncertainty as they attempt to use physical evidence, which happens to have survived and happens to have been discovered, to understand past human societies with many of which they have no other contact. Little wonder that archaeologists have become so concerned about theoretical issues and that even the least theoretical of archaeological writing is liberally sprinkled with the words 'probably', 'possibly', 'perhaps' and other qualifying words and phrases. In short, archaeologists face an epistemological problem: how do they know what they claim to know? Or, as Gosden (1992: 803) put it, 'Is what we write right'? Inevitably, this doubt influences the way that the subject is written about. There have even been those who have claimed that 'The past does not exist', except as a mental construct that each one of us has and that differs from person to person (Reid and Lane 2004: 1). For some who are inclined to postmodernism, this has become a justification for writing fictional accounts of the past (for example, parts of McIntosh 1998 and Joyce et al. 2002: 149–150). Such invention might seem extreme, but when handled with care it can be a valuable way of bringing the past to life for the reader. As indicated by the passage from Wheeler's *Maiden Castle* quoted in Chapter 2, it is actually not a new idea (Wheeler 1943: 62). Nevertheless, an archaeological author needs to be cautious about adopting such an approach. As Paul Bahn has written, 'It is so tempting to project one's own constructs onto the mute data, and ultimately to invent new myths for the media – in effect, to produce prehistoric novels' (Bahn 2007: 1088).

Epochs and culture history

I have often been unhappy about what I regarded as 'formulaic thinking' and have resisted the temptation to interpret the past in terms of this or that 'ism'. In practice, however, all thinking is formulaic; that is to say, it is shaped by ideas of one sort or another even if they are not explicitly defined. To be able to write about the archaeological past we need structuring concepts or models, the latter long ago explained by David Clarke as 'pieces of machinery that relate observations to theoretical ideas' (Clarke 1972b: 1). For instance, one of the most persistent structuring concepts has been the 'three-age system', the epochalistic model conceived in early-nineteenth-century Europe that saw the prehistoric past in terms of a succession of Stone Age, Bronze Age, Iron Age and their subdivisions (Daniel 1943). So many archaeological writers have used this model for so long that for many readers it has taken on a reality of its own. In spite of the theoretical agonizing of the last half-century, epochalism is still alive and well in parts of what is known, rather strangely, as 'the Old World'. Its apologists claim that they retain it merely to provide a useful set of labels for past periods, apparently forgetting that what we call things influences how we think about them. As for the rest of the world, attempts by Eurocentric archaeologists to apply the model to African archaeology have produced little more than confusion, whereas in the Americas or Australasia it has been irrelevant. Even in parts of the world where the model is still in common use, it needs to be accepted that, for example, there never was actually such a thing as 'the Bronze Age'. The problem is that the idea of the three-age system is now so deeply entrenched in public thinking that some archaeological writers have been trapped in an anachronistic mindset, at times without even realizing it. Long ago Glyn Daniel warned, 'This system has indeed been the foundation stone of modern archaeology; it is for us to say whether it is to become a mill-stone hanging around the necks of future archaeologists' (Daniel 1943: 60). It appears that some people were not paying attention.

The three-age system was developed when the central concern of archaeologists was with dating and with change through time. It also accorded well with the progressivist, stadial thinking that was then so general. However, from the middle of the twentieth century onwards, as radiocarbon and other forms of absolute dating contributed more detailed and more reliable chronologies, the epochal model ceased to be necessary. Nevertheless, in the first half of that century it had provided the time dimension for the mosaic of archaeological 'cultures' that were perceived as constituting the spatial element of the prehistoric past, particularly in Europe. The idea of the archaeological culture, basically a grouping of material evidence consistently found together, was largely promoted by the writings of Gordon Childe (e.g., Childe 1927), who drew on the ideas of Gustaf Kossinna in early-twentieth-century Germany. It was adopted by many European archaeologists of Childe's generation, who often attempted to combine it with elements of the three-age system. With the

addition of stratigraphic evidence from excavated sites and typo-
logical studies of artefact assemblages and their associations, it
became possible to construct a 'culture history' of the pre-literate
past. This culture-historical model was employed widely prior
to about 1960, although it developed along rather different lines
in America where Alfred Vincent Kidder was apparently one of
its early promoters (Webster 2008). Indeed, it is still used in some
parts of the world. For instance, since the early 1990s German
archaeologists have defined a 'Gajiganna Culture', belonging to
the 'Final Stone Age', for the first and second millennium BC
of northeastern Nigeria (Breunig, Garba and Hambolu 2001;
Wendt 2007). In its heyday, the culture-historical approach provided a useful structuring concept for archaeological authors
who were writing syntheses of the past, which could be presented
as a succession of cultures defined in terms of their artefacts and
their geographical distributions, each culture rather vaguely representing a distinct society or group of people (e.g., Piggott 1954).
Unfortunately, like the three-age system, in time the archaeological culture and its American equivalents became endowed
with a spurious reality and in addition encouraged a descriptive
empirical approach to the past that eventually proved sterile.

Discovering how people lived

However, some archaeologists envisioned a past that was more
than successive assemblages of pots and other artefacts. In
Britain, for instance, Grahame Clark pioneered an economic
and ecological approach to the prehistoric past of Europe.
One of his best-known syntheses consisted of ten chapters of
which the titles were as follows: Ecological zones and economic
stages; Catching and gathering: inland; Catching and gathering:
coastal and maritime; Farming: clearance and cultivation; Farming: crops and livestock; Houses and settlements; Technology:
stone, bronze, iron; Technology: other handicrafts; Trade; and
Travel and transport (Clark 1952: xi). Significantly the book
was titled *Prehistoric Europe: The economic basis*. Clearly, Clark
thought of the millennia that were his subject in terms of how
people had lived, rather than as an artefact-punctuated timetable.
Moreover, Clark was not alone in seeking a new way of visual-
izing the archaeological past. As early as 1948 Walter W. Taylor

in the United States was pleading for changes and, significantly, commending Clark's work (Taylor 1983: 170).

Nevertheless, I suspect that only those who first came to archaeology during or before the 1950s can fully appreciate the sudden and rapid changes in thinking that took place after that time. Arguably, these changes were the result of structural alterations within the discipline and in its relationship to society as a whole. Before the beginning of the 1960s professional archaeological employment was extremely rare; in Britain, for instance, it was limited to a handful of academics and museum workers. People of my generation were repeatedly told by our elders that a private income was necessary in order to be an archaeologist and that it was wise to take a degree in history or geography rather than archaeology, so that one could become a school teacher and pursue one's archaeological interests in one's spare time. In spite of the efforts of Clark and a few other archaeologists, this situation fostered conservative thinking; it was apparent how the discipline had got to where it was at, but it was not really clear how it was going to move forward. Only a few archaeologists might have foreseen what was to come, as paradigm shifts and radiocarbon dating made much of the previous work redundant. The theoretical and methodological ferment that followed in the 1960s and 1970s produced major changes in the way that archaeology was done and in the way that it was written about. Dubbed rather arrogantly but accurately the New Archaeology, the basic cause of these developments was surely the extraordinary expansion in archaeological employment during this period, particularly in universities. This resulted in the appearance of a large number of mostly young professional archaeologists who, unlike their predecessors, felt themselves freed by radiometric and other absolute dating techniques from the former preoccupation with chronology. Also unlike many of their predecessors, they had been formally trained in archaeology and were understandably critical of previous attempts to explain why and how change had occurred in human societies during the past. In particular, they questioned the role of migration and diffusion that until then had frequently been advanced as major causes of change. Instead, they sought new explanations.

The archaeological thinking that developed during the 1960s and 1970s had many strands but has been characterized by

the name 'processualism', referring to 'the search for regulari-
ties and generalizable developments in cultural dynamics across
space and through time' that characterized much of the writing
(Watson 2008: 29). Some archaeologists went so far as to seek
overall rules of human behaviour. There was a strong interest
in human ecology and adaptation to environment and a considerable growth in settlement studies. Cultural anthropology and
ethnology became more influential. The physical and biological sciences were drawn on heavily to broaden the spectrum of
evidence for past societies: subsurface prospection of sites, petro-
logical sourcing of stone artefacts, faunal analysis of food waste,
archaeobotanical study of plant gathering and domestication,
palaeoanthropological investigation of human skeletal material –
these and many other activities were often not new but they
became increasingly important. The nature of the archaeological
record was also questioned, leading to studies of site-formation
processes, garbage accumulation and taphonomy. In addition,
the analysis and presentation of archaeological data employed
a widening range of statistical analyses, made more accessible
by steadily improving access to computers and the availability of suitable software. As a result, many archaeologists of the
1960s and 1970s thought of their work as more 'scientific' than
the old culture-historical approach of their predecessors, whose
views at times they openly derided. Typically they stressed the
importance of research design based on hypothesis testing and
on deductive rather than inductive reasoning. On occasion they
even suggested that most of the archaeological research con-
ducted by earlier generations was worthless. These and many
other characteristics of processualism were most extensively
developed in the United States, famously associated with Lewis
Binford and Kent Flannery. However, the impact of processualism was also felt more widely, most notably in Britain with the
work of David Clarke that was cut short by his tragically early
death. In that same country during the 1960s and early 1970s
there was also the distinctive research of Eric Higgs (Higgs 1972,
1975), whose emphasis on an economic interpretation developed
from the earlier work of Grahame Clark and inspired a number
of archaeologists just embarking on their careers.

    As has often been the case when new ideas are promoted,
the claims made by some processualists were so extreme that
they were ultimately found to be unsustainable. Nevertheless,

processualism was instrumental in bringing about fundamental changes in the way that archaeology was done, even though those changes became attenuated and diluted by the time they reached some remoter parts of the world. For instance, although far removed from the full blast of processualist thinking by my field research in Nigeria, nevertheless some of it filtered through to me as I sweated in Benin City and in the Lake Chad area during my excavations in the 1960s. In spite of an immediate requirement to establish basic stratified chronological sequences where none existed, I found myself also interested in human responses to the environment, subsistence economy, settlement character, site-formation processes, ethnographic analogies and other aspects of the new approaches to archaeology. Contemporaries and near contemporaries of mine, flung to the far corners of the globe by a centrifugal quest for employment, were also influenced by processualism, in other parts of Africa, in Australia, in New Zealand and elsewhere. Even the 'classical archaeologists' who studied Greece and Rome, and who were regarded by many other archaeologists as notoriously conservative, were affected by the wind of change that blew even into the dusty corners of the discipline (e.g., Alcock and Osborne 2007).

Inevitably, the changes in archaeology during the 1960s and 1970s influenced the way that the subject was written about. There was a move away from writing that was mainly descriptive to what might be loosely called explanatory writing. Not only was the latter more difficult to do well but also those doing the writing were often relatively inexperienced authors or authors with a 'scientific' rather than a 'literary' background. All too frequently the result was prose that was turgid and opaque, as well as being laced with jargon and other words used in a specialized sense, usually without an adequate explanation of either. Often the reader found parts of the more specialized publications difficult to understand. In extreme cases reading such material became mental torture, the physical equivalent of which I often described as rolling naked in broken glass. The basic problem seemed to be that many archaeological authors were failing to grasp that they needed literary skills as well as archaeological ones. So much was this the case that at times even the most basic errors were committed. On one occasion in the 1960s I was asked by a colleague to read and comment on a paper that was about to be submitted to a journal. When I did so I found that it was nearly 10,000 words long, mainly it seemed because of a laboured and verbose style. I suggested some tight editing, but was told by the writer rather coldly that I clearly misunderstood what was necessary and that anyway the journal editor was expecting a paper of about that length!

Nevertheless, some authors during this period overcame the problems of archaeological writing with great skill. Kent Flannery and James Deetz immediately come to mind (e.g., Deetz 1977; Flannery 1982). To their work might be added the publications of Bruce Trigger, although he distanced himself from the New Archaeology to some extent (Trigger 1978: vii–xii). At the more general and textbook level, Brian Fagan was also deservedly successful (e.g., Fagan [1974–2007] had twelve editions in thirty-four years). In addition, during the 1960s and 1970s there was an extraordinary increase in the number of archaeological publications. Countless journal papers appeared, new journals were launched, edited volumes proliferated, syntheses multiplied. Compared with the 1950s there were many more additions to the disciplinary literature, even if some of them had little impact or were quickly forgotten. This expansion in publication was partly the consequence of an increasing number of university archaeology departments in many parts of the world. Their staffs not only produced their own publications but they also trained the next generation of archaeologists who in turn became authors. In addition, both staff and students formed part of an expanding market for archaeological publications, the contents of which were in turn fed back into teaching and research. Furthermore, there were many university graduates who had studied archaeology, often with other disciplines, who did not enter the archaeological profession but nevertheless contributed to an expansion in public interest in archaeology in some Western countries. Although largely fuelled by television, this expansion again increased the market for archaeological publications, particularly at the more popular level.

Diversification and introspection

By the 1980s enthusiasm for processualism was waning, although it has remained influential in many places, particularly in the United States. Some archaeologists were seeking to free themselves from an approach that in their opinion treated human societies as merely laboratory specimens reacting to ecological and other external stimuli. As one archaeologist put it to me some years later, it had been forgotten that there is such a thing as human choice; human beings can make individual decisions, even at times decisions that are not in their best interests. As the focus on processualist ideas diminished, there developed, particularly in Britain, what has been called 'post-processual archaeology', an approach difficult to define, even for specialists in theory. Some have characterized this movement as one that sought to put the individual back into archaeology, although Shanks regards such a description as a 'caricature'. Rather, he sees post-processual archaeology as including 'neo-Marxian anthropology, structuralism, various influences of literary and cultural theory, feminism, post-positivist social science, hermeneutics, phenomenology, and many others' (Shanks 2008: 133). He identifies some of its characteristics as 'constant questioning and critical scepticism; working with the indissoluble articulation of past and present in the archaeological project; asking how we can understand cultural difference, past and present; imagining that difference' (Shanks 2008: 142). Ian Hodder and Christopher Tilley have been closely associated with this approach, and the former also with 'symbolic archaeology'. Yet another development has been that of 'cognitive archaeology' (Renfrew 1982: 2). Indeed, archaeological thinking has continued to change, and some theorists now regard post-processualism as a thing of the past. However, perhaps we are too close to the most recent work to be able to see how various current ideas relate to one another. Overall, it appears that both post-processual and subsequent approaches to archaeology represent an increasingly sophisticated quest for information about the past, as well as promoting introspection about the interpretation of the material basis of that information. Archaeologists are increasingly pushing the boundaries of the images they create, perhaps at times pushing them further than they can be made to go.

Unfortunately, post-processualism and other recent theoretical stances have not led to greater clarity in writing. At times it has been characterized by 'obfuscatory and introverted arguments that have decreasing reference to problems of interest about the past' (Yoffee and Sherratt 1993: 1). The concepts involved are often difficult to explain, and there is a real danger that some readers will overlook important issues because they have been presented in what is perceived to be an incomprehensible way. The esoteric character of much theoretical discussion can also stimulate negative reactions, particularly from the more pragmatic archaeologists working as archaeological consultants, who in some countries now greatly outnumber the academic archaeologists from whom much of the theory emanates. There is the danger of an increasing gulf between those who actually 'do' archaeology, whether in the field, the laboratory or in publication, and those who quite legitimately think about what is done and how it might be done better. Even some of those in the academic sector have had their misgivings about the continual changes that have taken place in archaeological theory. Thus, 'In order to succeed as scholars in archaeology, young academics feel they must break through with a brand-new theory that overturns everything that came before it' (Bentley and Maschner 2008: 4). Also, 'the attraction to each generation of displacing their teachers by moving the intellectual goalposts is a good deal easier than building on past work to sharpen and improve it, which offers less easy fame and an uneasy dependence on older scholars' (Bintliff 2008: 155). As Bintliff further remarks, archaeological theory over the last half-century has been regarded as 'a stadial evolutionary ladder of development (rather ironic considering the critique of stadialism by post-processualists)'. This view, in which more sophisticated theories replaced more primitive ones, is now being rejected by some archaeologists (Bintliff 2008: 161). Indeed, it has been suggested that 'one of the most fruitful ways forward in archaeological theory is to recognize that all the approaches are useful and they all have something relevant to contribute. We must not fall into the trap where our theory is more important than what we learn from using it' (Bentley and Maschner 2008: 5).

This suggests that the way we do our archaeology and the way we write about it can vary depending on the sort of research questions that are being addressed. Thus it might be argued that there is no 'right' or 'wrong' theoretical approach but only different approaches. However, at any particular time some of these will fall into disuse or be explicitly rejected, because they are based on concepts that are no longer acceptable due to changed thinking in our own society. Thus, 'archaeologists don't so much discover the past as produce accounts of it; their attention is drawn as much to contemporary values and attitudes as to the past itself' (Shanks 2008: 137).

Conclusion

At one time most archaeologists saw their interpretations as 'reconstructions' of the past (e.g., Branigan 1974), and reconstruction art was symptomatic of this perception (Sorrell 1981). Increasingly we have come to realize that what we actually produce are 'constructions'. When we write about archaeology we have to turn data into text, and this task requires that we construct images of the past, images that will inevitably reflect the times we live in. Back in 1962, I was forcibly reminded that not everyone will move with the times when the veteran British archaeologist Mortimer Wheeler visited one of my excavations in Benin City, in Nigeria. Standing on the edge of a deep cutting he suddenly remarked, 'In Pakistan I had civilization stratified on civilization; here you have barbarism stratified on barbarism.' I found myself unable to reply; apart from what I considered as the offensive nature of a statement that might have been overheard by my Nigerian staff, it was difficult for me to accept that anyone could still think in terms of such outdated social evolutionism. Perhaps it was only intended as a joke and it was merely my sense of humour that was deficient. If so, nobody laughed.

Five

The process of writing

*10 percent inspiration,
90 percent perspiration*

The aim of every writer is to be read; otherwise why bother to do it? Writing is an almost magical means of communication, in which groups of signs are used to transfer information, ideas and arguments from the mind of one person to that of another. It really is amazing that it ever succeeds; the sad fact is that it often does not. A major difficulty is that the manner in which we write varies from individual to individual and of course varies according to the subject matter, just as the ways in which we read and talk also differ. Bacon's advice from more than four centuries ago still deserves our attention: 'Reading maketh a full man, conference a ready man, and writing an exact man' (Bacon 1909 [1597]: 159). With apologies for his sixteenth-century sexism, it seems that he thought that the three activities of reading, discussing and writing are closely related. Certainly one needs to read widely and critically to be able to write well, whereas talking with others is a good way to sort out ideas about one's writing, and the writing itself demands precision. Each of these activities requires intellectual effort, and the way that we write is a reflection of the way that we think; indeed perhaps writing can be regarded as fossilized thoughts. If those thoughts are confused, then one's writing will also be confused.

There are many books that tell one how to write, and some of them can be of considerable assistance with the details (of which Strunk and White 2000 is one of my favourites). However, the basic task of writing is one that each of us must tackle individually, because we all think differently, depending on our education, our experience, our personality and on other matters. It is virtually impossible to provide a recipe for successful writing that will suit everybody. The best way to learn how to write is to write, as often as possible and in as many forms as possible. My generation had the advantage of attending school at a time when the 'composition' or 'essay' was a favoured instrument of education (or, in our opinion at the time, of torture). Almost as soon as we were able to string words together into a sentence we found ourselves ordered to produce such pieces of writing on a variety of subjects. A friend of mine in Britain, for example, still has an essay written by him at the age of nine or ten (in the 1940s) entitled 'What I did on my holidays', preserved no doubt by a doting mother rather than by himself! School teachers nowadays tell me that the writing of essays is no longer a common practice, and certainly when I was still teaching undergraduates I sometimes came across students who claimed not to know what an essay was. This is a pity because constant essay writing – at Cambridge in the 1950s I produced one and sometimes two a week – proved in my case to be a sound preparation for subsequent writing for publication. Thus the process of learning how to write is one of constant practice and constant experimentation; basically one is teaching oneself how to do it. In the process it should become easier and easier, and in this respect I am reminded of the principle of 'Fairbairnism', once (and perhaps still) familiar to sporting oarsmen. Steve Fairbairn (1862–1938) was an Australian who became a noted Cambridge oarsman and rowing coach. One of the sayings attributed to him was, 'If you can't do it easy, you can't do it at all' (Collins Persse 1981). This slogan could equally be applied to writing: each of us must find the easy way to do it, but for each of us the easy way might be different.

Overall structure

The first thing to consider when undertaking a piece of writing is structure. This will vary depending on the purpose of the writing; for instance, whether it is a research monograph, a journal paper, a scholarly synthesis or a 'popular' book. However, whatever the case, the structure needs to be designed in such a way that it will most effectively communicate what it is that you wish to get across to the reader. Your central argument or ideas or information content should form the backbone of the chosen structure and the structure is best decided before you begin to write. This is not to deny that in the course of writing you might subsequently find it necessary to modify the structure, but to commence writing without one is akin to groping one's way into a darkened room. Personally, I prefer to plan the piece of writing in some detail, identifying component chapters, subheadings and even paragraphs, according to the requirements of what is to be written. This provides me with a skeleton before I write, and as I write I add the organs, the muscles, the circulatory system and other soft tissues. I even go so far as to select a title for the writing project before I start; it helps to focus my mind on what I am trying to do. Preferably, I set out the structure on paper before starting to write, but I have now been writing for so long that I confess that in my haste to get started I often just keep it in my head. This is not to be recommended because it risks disaster, a risk that increases as the size of the piece of writing being undertaken increases. I like to think of this in terms of boat and ship building. If writing a journal paper could be compared to building a yacht, then writing a full-length book is similar to constructing an ocean liner. Without careful and detailed planning before construction commences, there is a danger of work reaching the deck only to discover that there is a problem with the keel. In the case of a yacht this might prove expensive to rectify but not impossible; in the case of an ocean liner the shipyard could go bankrupt. There are many pieces of published writing where a close inspection reveals a weakness or even a failure in the structural design.

The structure adopted for a piece of writing decides the way that the writing is done, but the way that one writes affects the form of the structure. The writer needs to be continually aware of this interaction if it is to be kept under control. It is difficult to generalize, but writers of nonfiction, such as archaeologists, can structure their writing in a number of different ways. For example, some adopt what might be called a 'mosaic' approach, piecing together the relevant information to produce a rather dense text that might be well organized but is often laborious to read. The result can be so concentrated that I often compare it to instant coffee; it expands considerably with the hot water of the reader's attention. With the usual addition of in-text referencing or superscript numbering for footnotes or endnotes, this sort of writing is more suitable for selective piecemeal reading than for total consumption. The typical textbook often takes this form (but some general books also, e.g., Hall 2007), with the components of the text rigorously marshalled under a hierarchy of headings and subheadings and with the addition of 'boxes' of extra information on selected topics and of lengthy illustration captions (e.g., Scarre 2005). Seemingly designed for readers with a short attention span, it is doubtful if such books are ever read from cover to cover or, indeed, that they are ever meant to be. I suspect that authors adopting this approach tend to write in a similarly mosaic fashion, piecing together bits of text like a vast jigsaw. Years ago I was told of an archaeological author whose technique consisted of writing separate pieces of information onto numerous file cards that were then shuffled into various alternative orders, of which the most suitable was reproduced as a typescript. In these days of word processors, I suspect that there are writers who use their cut-and-paste function in a similar manner. It is certainly one way of writing, and for some subjects and particular publications it is perhaps the most appropriate.

Other writers employ what amounts to a 'narrative' approach (e.g., Deuel 1969). The narrative is a structure particularly suitable for general monographs written for nonarchaeological readers, but it can also be used in a range of other archaeological writing. Storytelling is perhaps as old as humanity, was an important part of the oral traditions of many non-literate societies in the recent past and figures in some of the world's greatest literature. Everyone likes a good story. However, the archaeological writer who adopts this structure has to remember that a story needs a beginning that must catch the reader's attention, a middle that must systematically relate the sequence of events or examine the subject in an ordered manner and an end to clinch the matter. The beginning is particularly important; the first sentence or paragraph of a piece of writing, be it a journal paper, or a book chapter or whatever, is what Fagan calls the 'hook', the means of enticing the reader into the story (Fagan 2006a: 41). Experienced writers, like experienced lecturers, know how important an opening statement is and accept that it must be positive, not negative, and never apologetic. The first sentence of the present chapter is an example of such a hook. Another aspect of major concern with the narrative structure is continuity, so that each part of the text flows on into the next. The writer adopting a mosaic structure can stack up the components of the subject like bricks, with or without mortar to hold them together, but working with a narrative structure is like growing a tree, whose roots, stem, branches and leaves are interdependent. It follows that the actual writing needs to be a continuous process and perhaps is best done in as few work sessions as possible, even though much time might be spent on subsequent revision. In contrast to the construction that characterizes writing with a mosaic approach, the adoption of a narrative structure requires the development of more literary skills and the outcome should be more readable.

A third type of structure commonly used in nonfiction writing is the 'argument' approach (e.g., Hiscock 2008). It is particularly appropriate in scholarly works, such as journal papers, but is by no means confined to them. It is employed in a lot of archaeological writing, especially in the presentation and interpretation of fresh evidence or the reexamination of previous evidence and interpretations. As already stated, a central argument or ideas or information content should form the backbone of any structure that is adopted, but with the argument approach the argument itself becomes the structure. To use it effectively, clarity of expression and a carefully ordered logical presentation are essential. It is also more likely to succeed if the opening premise and the concluding statement are related; that is to say, a closely argued piece of writing will turn back on itself so that it finishes where it began. I often think of this as the head biting the tail, but in reality it is the other way round! Furthermore, although paragraph and sentence structure need care in all writing, as discussed later, they need the very greatest attention when the argument approach is used. In addition, appropriate word choice should be a major concern; many a published argument has been weakened by overstatement or ostentatious language or sometimes even by the reverse. The writer who employs the argument structure must aim not only to be read but also to convince.

I have tried to identify three main structures that archaeologists and, indeed, many other writers of nonfiction routinely employ. Readers might find my characterization too subjective or even idiosyncratic, and in that case I invite them to make their own analysis of relevant writing structures. They might identify important approaches that I have overlooked, and they will almost certainly find that hybrid structures also exist, where writers have used a mixture of approaches. In addition, there are often cases where an author will switch from one approach to another during the course of a piece of writing, particularly if it is a large project like a book. Furthermore, it has to be recognized that some writers will go about their task in blissful ignorance of formal structure and cobble their text together in whatever way seems appropriate or easiest. If it succeeds in its task, why not? Sometimes others will find a piece of writing readable and interesting, but its author will be unable to understand how this was achieved.

Paragraph and sentence structure

However, whether or not a writer adopts what might be called a 'macrostructure', of the sort discussed earlier, close attention to the 'microstructure' of a piece of writing will be essential. For example, the paragraph structure is a vital organizational tool that should be so designed that it leads the reader through the text step by step. Each paragraph should deal with a separate part of the subject in a way that enables readers to look at it and say, this is about such a matter. Indeed, when writing, it is worth repeatedly asking oneself what the purpose of each paragraph is and what it is contributing. Some writers worry about paragraph length, but that is not as important as achieving integrity for paragraph content. The start of a new paragraph should tell the reader that there is a change in the subject, and the sequence of paragraphs should provide an overall framework for the piece of writing, whether it is a paper or a chapter or other subdivision of a book. Nevertheless, I try to avoid paragraphs longer than about 400 words, and paragraphs shorter than about 200 words are more appropriate to journalism than to the sort of writing discussed here. Short paragraphs might be helpful to the standing commuter reading a newspaper on a swaying train to the city, but in the writing that archaeologists have to do they can seriously fragment continuity. In practice that continuity can be one of the more difficult aspects of paragraph writing. Paragraphs have the job of breaking up the subject into digestible bits, but it is nevertheless necessary for each paragraph to lead on to the next, so that the reader's attention is carried onwards without too much disruption. This continuity can be achieved if the first sentence of a new paragraph alludes in some way to the last sentence of the previous paragraph. The briefest way of doing this is by using a 'connective', 'a linguistic form that connects words or word groups' (Merriam-Webster 2001: 244). Connectives are also relevant to the subject of sentence structure discussed next. Frequently used ones include the following: however, therefore, nevertheless, moreover, furthermore, as well as various phrases such as: in spite of that, another aspect is, in addition, since then. These are a few examples only; the creative writer will also find other ways of maintaining continuity between paragraphs.

If more care is often needed in the construction of paragraphs, far greater attention is necessary to the task of building and connecting sentences. Most writers are now sensitive to the problem of the overlong sentence, in which the reader gets lost before the end is reached. Nineteenth-century authors seem to have loved the long sentence; it gave respectability in an age when that quality was valued above many others. In Chapter 2, for instance, I mentioned a sentence of Belzoni's that consisted of ninety-three words (Belzoni 1971 [1820]: 259), but a search of modern archaeological publications might well reveal similar monsters. One authority on English usage called such sentences 'trailers': 'the sort of sentence that tires the reader out by again and again disappointing his [or her] hope of coming to an end', and added that 'the trailer style is perhaps of all styles the most exasperating' (Fowler 1965: 645). So, beware the long sentence: it can strain your punctuation skills and still result in unreadable prose. Of almost equal concern, however, is the other extreme. The writer addicted to short sentences risks producing prose that is fired at the poor reader like bursts from a machine gun. The basic problem, of course, is how to define a sentence. Fowler supplied no less than ten definitions (1965: 546) and even discussed 'verbless sentences' (1965: 674–676), which in my ignorance I used to think were invented by first-year undergraduates who didn't know any better. Here I sense the danger of being drawn into a minefield of grammatical detail that many other writers have dealt with (I rely on Carey 1960; Fowler and Fowler 1962; Fowler 1965). I have bitter memories of school exercises of many years ago, in which we were made to 'analyse' endless sentences and were expected to be able to identify subject and predicate, transitive and intransitive verbs, conditional clauses, adjectival clauses, participles, adverbs, pronouns, conjunctions and so on. It is possible that this was very good for us, but it is certain that most of us quickly forgot it, even those of us who subsequently became authors of one sort or another. My business here is merely to alert archaeological writers to the main problems of sentence construction that can so fundamentally affect readability.

The construction of sentences also requires the punctuation skills that have already been mentioned. Use of a range of punctuation will make it easier for the reader to grasp the intended meaning of a sentence and will contribute to continuity within each sentence. Everyone knows that a sentence begins with a capital letter and ends with a full stop (a period in America), but it takes some practice to be able to use commas wisely and it has been claimed that correct use of the semi-colon is an indication of an experienced writer. There is also the colon, so useful at the beginning of a list; the apostrophe, which is frequently misused; the hyphen, so often applied inconsistently; the question mark, whose use should be limited; and the exclamation mark that is best avoided except on rare occasions. Other forms include inverted commas (quotation marks) and the decision to use single or double ones, with the alternative used for quotations within quotations; brackets, both round and square; and the dash, now so often used instead of more appropriate punctuation and repeatedly confused with the en-rule. Attention is also needed to other writing devices, such as the appropriate use of italics and bold, the ellipsis and the stroke (the slash in America) and of that handy Latin term *sic* (usually located in square brackets). This is not the place to discuss these matters in detail, but the beginning archaeological author would be wise to investigate them in the copious reference literature that exists, such as the *Style manual: For authors, editors and printers* (2002) or *The Oxford style manual* (Ritter 2003). Furthermore, the opinion of G. V. Carey (1960: 1) on the subject of punctuation is worth bearing in mind: 'To say that no two persons punctuate exactly alike would no doubt be an exaggeration, but most people would probably agree that punctuation is a matter not only of rules but of personal taste'.

In addition, as with continuity between paragraphs, there is a need for sentence continuity. The prose must carry the reader on from sentence to sentence with as little effort as possible. Sudden changes of subject will prevent this, and in particular the *non sequitur*, Latin for 'it does not follow', should be avoided (Allen 1990: 807). Here again, as with paragraphs, connectives can save the day, but some words, for example 'also', should be used sparingly if tedious repetition is to be prevented. Indeed, word repetition of any sort can be a problem, particularly in the same sentence. Except perhaps for rhetorical purposes, it is best avoided; it often results in dull and ugly prose. Use of a synonym dictionary can be of assistance in such cases, and Roget's *Thesaurus*, first published in 1852, is still worth consulting at times (Kirkpatrick 1998).

Word choice, expression, spelling and measurements

This brings us to the important subject of word choice (on which see Orwell 1946). Personally, I prefer to use simple language that can be readily understood by as wide a range of readers as possible. Some of them will not have English as their first language, and even within the English-speaking world there are, for example, differences of usage among Britain, the United States, Australia and elsewhere. In my own writing, for instance, 'shapeless' might be preferred to 'amorphous', 'difference' to 'dichotomy', 'glassy' to 'vitreous', 'at the same time' to 'synchronous', 'do' to 'operationalize' and so on. As Strunk and White expressed it, 'Do not be tempted by a twenty-dollar word when there is a ten-center handy, ready and able' (2000: 76–77). However, simplicity can be difficult to attain when writing about a discipline that has a tendency to invent words or to borrow terms from other social sciences, so that words such as 'discourse', 'ontology', 'heuristic', 'dialectic', 'hermeneutic', 'agency', 'structuration' and 'reflexivity' are in use. Therefore, every effort needs to be made to explain the meaning of words that are legitimate specialized terms and to avoid using those that are merely jargon. This task will seem tedious and unnecessary to many writers but it is important that not only writers know what they mean; as many readers as possible must also know and frequently this is not the case. As an archaeological writer, you need to avoid the accusation of writing 'prose so obscure and tortuous that nobody, including yourself, is quite sure at the end of it what you have been saying' (Bahn 1989: 37). It is also the case that:

> Complicated diction and fashionable vocabulary may impress in the short term, but they ensure that, in the long run, the ideas will be forgotten. Even worse, by introducing bogus jargon into our own published writing, we run the risk of spreading these poorly-understood ideas through future generations of publications and research.... Muddled language not only muddles our current understanding of things, but it also multiplies itself and infects academic thought in the future. (Bentley 2006: 200)

In matters of expression as well as word choice, considerable care is necessary. 'Language is about communication, and well-chosen language makes for clear communication' (Chippindale 1996: 54). It is wise, for instance, to avoid fashionable or 'vogue' phrases, such as those common in the popular media or in everyday speech. Examples might include 'low profile', 'steep learning curve', 'boxing oneself into a corner', 'any time soon', 'no stranger to' and 'showcase their skills'. Not only are such expressions ugly and verbose but also like a lot of popular language and slang they tend to be short-lived and sometimes regionally specific. It is pointless using expressions that might not be familiar to readers in twenty years or in a different part of the world. Equally, it is important not to overwrite; as Strunk and White insisted: 'Vigorous writing is concise. A sentence should contain no unnecessary words ... [make] every word tell' (2000: 23). This is a matter that merits close attention during revision, as discussed later. Also there is the danger of overstatement; archaeological writers seem to be particularly prone to this problem, and it can cause the reader to lose confidence in a writer's judgement. The words 'probable', 'possible', 'perhaps' and 'very' need to be used with care, whereas few archaeological discoveries or publications are actually 'exciting' or 'fascinating'. Similarly, it is unwise to write, 'it is extremely difficult to say', when even a reader on the verge of falling asleep can see that it is quite impossible. There is also the annoying habit of concluding the discussion of a probably unresolvable point by claiming that further research will be necessary, without giving the slightest indication of what form that research might take. Perhaps the most dangerous of expressions, however, is the unintentional howler, although it might enliven the text for the observant reader. A recent example was a paper that referred to 'the female womb', raising questions perhaps about male anatomy (Mégaloudi, Papadopoulos and Sgourou 2007: 937). Better still, I once had a student who wrote, 'Life was hard in Catal Huyuk but at least they had coarse mating on the floor'. Which brings us, of course, to the delicate subject of spelling.

Beginning writers in this wonderful age of word processors seem to think that they do not need to know how to spell because their computer will do it for them. To a point this is so, but I find myself alert to the problems of 'there' and 'their', 'alter' and 'altar', 'current' and 'currant', 'to' and 'too', 'whether' and 'weather', 'fare' and 'fair' and so on. Even if your software is clever enough to discriminate correctly in such cases, it is wise to keep a sharp eye on the matter. It is also important to remember where one's writing is to be published. Spelling in the United States famously differs from that in the United Kingdom, but in more numerous ways than is sometimes realized. One needs to set one's word processor to the spelling that is required; mine even gives me a choice of Australian spelling also, which mystifies me and I actually live in the country. Be that as it may, it is sensible to make sure that your text is spelt in the appropriate manner for the country of publication; editors on both sides of the Atlantic are apt to be unimpressed by incorrect spelling. It is also a good idea to have a copy of *The Concise Oxford Dictionary of Current English* and of the American *Merriam-Webster's Collegiate Dictionary* by one's side as one writes. Not only will they help to resolve uncertainties of spelling such as alternative forms but also they will be useful for checking meaning and usage that can sometimes vary in unexpected ways. The words that you use must mean what you intend them to mean, and this must be the case in as many English-speaking countries as possible.

While on this sensitive subject of international relations, there is also the matter of measurements. Continental Europe, Australia, Canada, New Zealand and almost every other country in the world have adopted the metric system, the 'International System of Units' (SI), as their primary or sole system of measurement. The United States, Liberia and Myanmar have not (Metric system 2008), and for incomprehensible reasons Britain has retained its mile. Thus, when writing for American editors and publishers, it is necessary to use the pre-metric system of feet and inches and so on that was inherited from the British, as well as stating the metric equivalents. Some editors will insist on the nonmetric measurement being given first, with the metric equivalent following in brackets; others will want it the other way round. Unless you want to have to alter everything to the desired form to please the editor, it is a good idea to get it right the first time.

To sum up this chapter so far, it seems to me that in the end writing is a performance, in this case an archaeological performance (see Shanks 2004 on archaeology and performance). In this respect it compares closely with lecturing. A really good lecturer (during a long career I have heard very few) will be at least equally concerned with presentation as with content. So it is with writing. You might be the greatest authority of all time about a particular aspect of archaeology, but this will amount to little if you are unable to write about it in an understandable and interesting way. In fact, there have been instances of greatly respected scholars who found writing so difficult that they published infrequently. At the other extreme there have been those that have poured out turgid, repetitive material that contributed little to archaeological scholarship. So, the quality of a written performance matters, and in the end that is judged by the extent to which the writer's aims are realized. Indeed, it has been claimed that performance and realization are the most effective ways of measuring the success of a piece of published work. However, it is now necessary to look at the nitty-gritty business of actually doing the writing.

The mechanics of writing

As indicated in the title of this chapter, writing needs inspiration, but it requires much more perspiration. The intending author would do well to look closely at Brian Fagan's comments on how he goes about it. As he says, 'The fact is that writing is a hard slog along the way, word after word, sentence after sentence, paragraph after paragraph. You've got to get words on paper' (Fagan 2006a: 92). He is absolutely right. Self-discipline and a schedule that is adhered to are essential. Like him, I set myself a target of 1,000 words a day, which I have discovered is the aim of many writers. On a bad day I might only produce 500 or so, but on a good day it might be as high as 1,200 or even 1,500. He insists that he sits there until he has done his daily quota (2006a: 96); I merely keep going until I run out of time or energy or both. However, I do keep a daily record of the number of words written so that I can monitor my progress. Also, at the beginning of a writing project I construct what I call a 'backwards timetable'; commencing at the intended submission date, it provides a plan of the work back to the present time, so that I can see at a glance the approximate date by which each part must be completed. In the past I sometimes worked eight hours a day for six-day periods, with a day's rest once a week, so that a full-length book of about 100,000 words could theoretically be completed in four to five months (but in practice took much longer); now my endurance is somewhat less. For most of us, of course, such a schedule is only possible during study leaves or vacations, but even a full-time job need not prevent one from following an organized writing programme. I now enjoy/endure the so-called advantages of retirement, but some years ago I managed to produce one of my books whilst also running a university department and carrying a full teaching load. I did it by rolling out of bed at 5.00 AM every weekday morning, sitting down with a large mug of tea and writing from 5.30 to 8.30 AM, then grabbing breakfast and getting to work by 9.00 AM; the evenings were reserved for assessing students' assignments and preparing teaching material. I am by no means the first person to have written in such a way (e.g., Shaw 1961: vi), and I am sure that I will not be the last. The harsh fact is that writing needs determination; except for the rare individual who *appears* to be able to do it without undue exertion, the rest of us have to sweat for it.

Many people deliberately write what they regard as a first draft, comforting themselves with the belief that they will be able to sort out its problems at the revision stage. I have always made myself believe that what I write is the way it is going to be, although I still revise the result, sometimes substantially. I have never liked the idea of producing a rough version that I might or might not have the time to put right later. This means that my writing is probably slower than that of some authors, but each of us has to find the way that we can best do things. I once knew an historian who insisted that he only aimed to write one paragraph a day but that the paragraph that he wrote would be in its final state and not need any revision. This is an extreme method that I would not advise. A problem that is frequently experienced is how to get going in the first place. Inexperienced writers often agonize about the first few sentences, feeling obligated to produce something impressive, and (as already discussed) Fagan's 'hook' at the beginning of a piece of writing can be useful (Fagan 2006a: 41). Nevertheless, the best way to begin is just to begin; very likely your opening passage will eventually be altered anyway, after you have completed the rest of the paper or book and can see the opening in its full context. However, as already mentioned, I do like to select a title for whatever I am writing *before* I start; it helps me to concentrate on what I am trying to do. Publishers tend to be concerned about book titles because they can affect sales; misleading or exaggerated ones can irritate journal editors. In my own case, it is titles containing puns or jokes that I find most annoying. One example that I recollect was a study of fish bones and stone artefacts from an Australian site that was called 'Fish and chips', but mercifully it was only an unpublished thesis. Certainly titles deserve a lot of thought, and brevity is worth aiming for, as anyone who has ever struggled with tediously verbose titles when constructing a list of references will surely agree. However, a very brief book title can cause a publisher to ask for an explanatory subtitle, which defeats the object of the exercise.

Also before starting to write, I find it essential to have a detailed plan of what I am about to do, as previously mentioned. The plan might well have to be modified as I proceed, but having one does help me to achieve a logical structure and to avoid omissions, repetitions and irrelevant digressions as I write. However, the actual task of writing can be greatly complicated by the data that form its raw material. The problem that this creates for the archaeological writer is comparable with that described by the historian E. H. Carr:

> The commonest assumption appears to be that the historian divides his work into two sharply distinguishable phases or periods. First, he spends a long preliminary period reading his sources and filling his notebooks with facts: then, when this is over, he puts away his sources, takes out his notebooks and writes his book from beginning to end. This is to me an unconvincing and unplausible picture. For myself, as soon as I have got going on a few of what I take to be the capital sources, the itch becomes too strong and I begin to write – not necessarily at the beginning, but somewhere, anywhere. Thereafter, reading and writing go on simultaneously. The writing is added to, subtracted from, re-shaped, cancelled, as I go on reading. The reading is guided and directed and made fruitful by the writing: the more I write the more I know what I am looking for, the better I understand the significance and relevance of what I find. (Carr 1961: 22–23)

Much of the writing that archaeologists do is rather different from that of the historian, and Carr's assumption that all historians are male was far from true even when he wrote but his comments are nevertheless relevant. We have to balance the job of writing against the job of accessing the data we need as we write, a requirement that is constantly changing. I would not necessarily adopt Carr's approach, although it might be useful when writing a general synthesis, and I do agree that one does not have to start writing at the beginning. Nevertheless, the huge mass of excavation or analysis data that forms the subject of much archaeological writing can be difficult to handle during the writing process. Each of us must find our own way of solving this issue, depending on the sort of writing in each case. We have to avoid endless correction and augmentation at the revision stage, when it is discovered that information has been overlooked, but also we have to avoid constant interruption to the business of writing.

Such interruptions can result in writing that is jerky and disjointed, so that readers quickly tire of it. What one needs is writing that flows easily, and each of us will have different ways of achieving this. In my case, I like to relax in isolation and comfort, shut away in my study at home surrounded by my files and papers. Others, I suspect, work best when under stress. Nowadays, we all sit in front of our word processor, but for those of us who have been writing for many years it was not always thus. People schooled in the 1940s learnt to write a conventional script, first in pencil, then with a steel nib and inkwell, finally with the luxury of a fountain pen. Inevitably many of us grew up able to think with a pen in our hand; in the days of mechanical and then electrical typewriters I never composed on them, because it was too difficult to alter things. Instead I wrote what was literally a manuscript, covered in corrections some of which were on bits of paper stuck to the appropriate page. I then typed this up and used the resulting typescript for revision purposes. Finally, I passed the corrected typescript to a professional stenographer who produced a 'clean' copy (I recollect that in 1978 Cambridge University Press was instructing its authors that every page of a submitted typescript must be free of corrections). In the event of last-minute changes, a whole page would need retyping or, worse still, a whole chapter if the changes displaced page breaks. In these respects, the word processor has been a godsend with its cut-and-paste functions and the means of constantly checking word length, although I am doubtful that it has improved the way people write. So now I operate a keyboard and give thanks for the Macintosh and for Microsoft Word. There is no longer an inked-stained callus on the middle finger of my right hand. Mind you there are some old-timers whom I know who refuse to give up their fountain pens, and excessive devotion to the keyboard can result in what has become known as RSI, or repetitive strain injury.

Nevertheless, interruptions to the process of writing can occur if one reaches a point where information needs to be verified or where more information is needed. It is fatal to stop writing in order to look for it. The chances are that you will not be able to find it and a half-hour later, when you get back to the writing, you will have forgotten what it was that you intended to say next. I have long dealt with this problem by having a manila file by my elbow labelled 'Problems'. Into it go notes of anything that I think needs further attention, and I continue writing without serious interruption. After I have finished the paper or chapter, I then burrow into my records or decamp to the library to sort the various problems out. Another disruptive business, of course, is referencing. Whether you prefer to reference using the Harvard System, as I do, or superscript numbers and footnotes or endnotes, pausing to find that pesky reference can be severely time wasting. It is better to file a note that it is needed, and then put the reference into the text at the end of the day or at an early revision stage, than to stop to look for it. It is absolutely essential to see every reference that is used, and this can take a lot of time and trouble. It has been claimed that 'most authors copy their references from other bibliographies [list of references] rather than reading the articles themselves' (Bentley 2006: 196). Such a practice is not only dishonest but can also perpetuate errors; if an original reference proves unobtainable, it should only be used in the text if it is included in the list of references as 'cited by' the source from which it came.

Concerning the list of references, it is important to build it up as one proceeds, day by day or chapter by chapter depending on the length of what is being written. In the past I did this on file cards; now I construct the list of references on the word processor, in a separate document from the text, and the search facility can ensure that the removal of an in-text reference and its entry in the list of references during revision will not leave a forgotten in-text reference without a source in the list. Indeed, many people now use the software known as 'EndNote', which constructs the referencing and list of references as one writes. It is therefore surprising how many incomplete or incorrect references and reference-list entries can still be found in postgraduate theses and even in published works. However, whatever method is adopted, it is unwise to leave the referencing and the reference list until the text is completed. Years ago I asked a student whose thesis submission date was only days away whether he was going to meet the deadline. 'No problem', he replied. 'It's finished; I've only got the referencing and the reference list to do.' Needless to say, my heart sank.

Collaborative writing

Much of the business of writing discussed earlier depends on personal choice, but we are not always writing alone. At times we find it necessary or advantageous to collaborate with one or more other writers. Now there might be those who think that collaboration is easier than working on one's own. This is not so; it takes quite a lot of experience to collaborate successfully. First of all, it must be decided how the collaboration is to function. Is one person to do all the research and the other to do all the writing, with both names being given as the authorship? Is one person to write a part of the text and the other another part of it, again under joint authorship but with an indication of who wrote which part? Alternatively, should one author write the text and pass it to the second author who revises, alters and adds to it before passing it back for further work by the first author? This can go on for some time and can wreck old friendships. An even riskier method is to sit side by side at the same computer and jointly decide on every phrase, clause and sentence. I once even collaborated on a paper (with Frank Willett) by sitting with a tape recorder between us, into which we read each sentence after we had decided what it should say. The tape was then given to his long-suffering secretary to transcribe on the typewriter. Surprisingly it even got published, although, hardly surprisingly, with a rather obvious misprint in it. There are probably other ways of collaborating that I have overlooked, and of course some collaborations have not two but three or four or more authors. *Antiquity* 76 (2002: 980–990) has a paper with no less than nineteen authors that I will excuse myself from referencing fully. One wonders how they did it: by sitting round a table and arguing for a week or by means of endless e-mails? In any event, collaboration creates yet another problem: in what order are the authors' names to appear? Some insist that alphabetical order is fairest: fine if your name is Adams, a problem if it is Williams. Others insist that the names should be arranged according to percentage input, but try to agree on that! Finally, there is still the individual whose name is put first because she or he is the professor, whereas the name of the postgraduate student who did most of the work is put second. The world was always a wicked place.

Conclusion

So you've finished writing, what then? You need to revise, probably several times over: cutting out every superfluous word, improving the expression, checking for errors or omissions, double-checking every in-text reference against the list of references and so on. This can be a very detailed task, during which it is recommended that the appropriate sections of a specialized text such as Matthews, Bowen and Matthews (2000) be consulted as a guide. It is also a good idea to refer to a general book on writing techniques, to help identify weaknesses of composition (one of my favourites is Osland et al. 1991). After that you need to put the text away 'for at least three weeks and then re-read it'. Many problems that you have overlooked 'will leap out of the page at you, and can be corrected' (White 1983: 172). Following this further revision (although some writers prefer to do it at an earlier stage), it is a good idea to ask several colleagues and friends to read what you have written, but choose them with care. A person who is uncritical will be of little value to you but one who is overcritical might cause you to make changes that are at best pedantic and at worst detrimental. However, comments that appear justified should be acted on so far as possible, resulting in still further revision. Your writing will still have to run the gauntlet of journal referees or publisher's readers and copy editors, so it is wise to deal with any perceived weaknesses before that happens. In the end, it is essential to make sure that what you have written is in the best possible state *before* it eventually goes to the printer. During the whole long process of revision one should remember the remark of the Roman writer Horace, more than 2,000 years ago, that 'what you publish you can no longer tear up' (Sisson 1975: 35).

Six

Visual explanation

Pictures that should talk

Back in the early 1970s I knew a university where the Faculty of Arts lecture theatres had no projection facilities of any sort. When it was pointed out that in lectures about archaeology it was necessary to use either slides or an overhead projector (this was long before PowerPoint was even thought of), one of the historians in the Faculty remarked that if one's lectures were any good one did not need pictures. The really disturbing thing about this comment was that I had the distinct impression that he was actually serious. I should perhaps apologize at this point to the vast majority of historians who clearly do appreciate the value of illustrations in what they write. However, it seems to have long been the case that archaeologists have had a greater need for and appreciation of visual images than historians. History, like most of the humanities, privileges text rather than pictures; after all most of its evidence is in the form of text. In contrast, archaeology, straddling the humanities and the natural sciences, has a fundamental requirement for a wide range of illustrative material. The subject is primarily concerned with physical evidence, with artefacts, with sites, with chemical analyses and so on; pictures in the widest sense of the word become essential. They can include photographs, photomicrographs, drawings of objects, maps, plans, excavation section drawings, histograms, a variety of technical diagrams and (although strictly speaking they are part of the text) tables of various sorts. The successful archaeological author must therefore be able to think in visual terms as well as in literary ones. To be able to write well is not enough. Nevertheless, again and again, archaeological publications appear with illustrations of poor quality, in spite of the remarkable technical advances in graphics and printing in recent years. Admittedly, editors, publishers and printers must bear some of the blame for this, but the basic responsibility lies with archaeological authors, some of whom are not sufficiently concerned about visual quality and overall relevance. Perhaps this inadequate concern has something to do with a deep-seated bias in Western education: text is what really matters; pictures belong in the kindergarten.

Instead, pictures should be regarded as a basic form of communication, along with speech and writing. Many years ago the British archaeologist Stuart Piggott, writing about archaeological draughtsmanship, had the following to say: 'All technical and scientific illustration is at once symbol and communication, a pictorial language addressing the author's audience side by side with his written text' (Piggott 1965: 165). Piggott knew what he was talking about; he was one of the best archaeological illustrators of his generation. Others were less skilled, and one of Piggott's contemporaries, Richard Atkinson, referred to what he called 'visual illiteracy' (Hope-Taylor 1966: 109). Indeed, there are people who appear to be unable to 'read' images and are therefore unlikely to create informative ones. Concerning archaeological illustrations, Atkinson also wrote, 'They provide a medium of description and record far more concise and more easily understood than many times the same amount of text, and if carefully planned will considerably lighten both the writer's and the reader's task' (Atkinson 1953: 185). In spite of the passage of time and innovations in illustrating that these writers could hardly have dreamed of, their remarks remain relevant: archaeological illustration is an integral part of archaeological writing, a vital aspect of achieving the author's basic task of communicating with the reader. As the online 'Notes for contributors' to the

Antiquaries Journal remarks, illustrations 'communicate to most people much more quickly and accurately than text' (*Antiquaries Journal* 2009). Perhaps it is only theoretical archaeologists and those specializing in numerical analysis who can sometimes do without illustrations, and even they need them at times. For almost every other sort of archaeologist, illustrations will be a major matter of concern and often of expense that can take just as long to attend to as the writing of the text. In coping with the problems that they present, the archaeological author will be faced with two main considerations: first, how to prepare the illustrations or otherwise obtain them; second, how to use them in the intended publication.

Photographs

Photographs have long been regarded as an important illustrative medium by archaeological authors. In the past nearly always in black and white, with colour only becoming common in recent times, photographs were frequently a cause of tension between writers and editors or publishers, because of printing costs that were greater than those for line drawings. This was the case when photographs had to be printed from half-tone blocks usually on glossy paper different from the text, in contrast to drawings that were printed from line blocks on the same paper as the text. With the revolutionary changes that have taken place in printing technology over the last few decades, this is no longer necessary, but photographs remain a little more expensive to reproduce than drawings and authors are still often limited in the number that they can include in a publication. Indeed, the greater cost of printing colour photographs means that they are particularly limited in number when they are used.

So far as the preparation of photographic illustrations is concerned, archaeological authors have usually taken their own photographs, although on larger excavations and fieldwork projects another member of the research team, and sometimes even a professional photographer, has often done the work instead. Perhaps the most famous of such professional photographers was M. B. Cookson, Mortimer Wheeler's photographer, one of the earlier specialists in archaeological photography (Cookson 1954). In particular, studio photography of artefacts or photomicrography has tended to be left to such professionals. The equipment favoured by archaeologists who took their own photographs has changed over the years, from the large-format plate cameras of the 1940s and before, to the twin-lens medium-format reflex cameras of the 1950s, to the single-lens 35-mm reflex cameras of the 1960s to 1990s (for which the development of the zoom lens was a godsend for excavators), to the digital cameras of the present time. This is not the place to consider the technical aspects of archaeological photography, on which many have written (e.g., Simmons 1969; Conlon 1973; Harp 1975; Lyons and Avery 1977; Beresford and St. Joseph 1979; Dorrell 1989; Howell and Blanc 1992), although digital cameras have now rendered much of this material outdated. However, some of the most important aspects of archaeological photography have more to do with the person holding the camera than with the camera itself. Many published examples of archaeological photographs betray a failure to make the best use of light and shadow or suffer from a poorly prepared subject, or an unsuitable angle of view, or poor composition, or a lack of a scale, or too many scales, or a careless focus or an incorrect exposure. In the past, a few problems could be remedied in the darkroom, where the processing of negatives and prints was often in the hands of professionals. Now, with digital technology, archaeologists can themselves do much more to improve an unsatisfactory image, but the fact remains that nothing really replaces careful thought at the time that the photograph is taken. It might sound obvious but the crucial thing for the archaeological photographer is to decide exactly what it is that she or he wants to show and then to determine how it can best be shown. For good archaeological photographs it is not enough to merely point the camera and press the button.

Drawings

Not only did my generation of archaeological authors believe that proficiency in photography was essential but we also realized that we had to learn how to draw our own maps, plans, sections, artefacts and other line illustrations, because only rarely would anybody else do it for us (methodological texts included: Grinsell, Rahtz and Warhurst 1966; Brodribb 1970; Griffiths, Jenner and Wilson 1990). In the field we drew at a large scale, so as to benefit from the increase in sharpness resulting from the reduction necessary for publication (Hope-Taylor 1967: 183). Later, back in our study, we raised Indian ink tracings of such drawings on draughting linen or, by the 1960s, on plastic film. These often proved difficult to reduce photographically for publication. Pottery and other artefacts were drawn full-sized and sometimes presented similar difficulties. There were no photocopiers of a size or sophistication that could produce satisfactory reductions. Our worst nightmare, however, was lettering; most drawings needed some, it often took as long to do as the line work had taken, and poor lettering was frequently the ruination of a good drawing. Archaeologists trained in art or calligraphy, or those who were merely courageous, could manage freehand lettering; the rest of us depended on plastic stencils, replaced in the 1960s by transfer lettering, and in the 1970s and 1980s by photographic or mechanical methods.

As with photography, it was digital technology that changed all this, and since the late 1980s computer-generated line illustrations, some of them downloaded from digital surveying equipment, have made life much easier. Indeed, geographic information systems have provided archaeologists with a sophisticated mapping capacity. Furthermore, a variety of software now exist that enable a wide range of other artwork to be prepared from scratch on the screen. However, building up the line work of a complex drawing on a computer screen can be laborious and can require the skills of a digital graphic artist, somewhat beyond those of many archaeologists. As a result, it is often quicker (and cheaper than employing a specialist) to do the line work in Indian ink on an A3 (420 × 297 mm) format, reduce it to A4 (297 × 210 mm) on a photocopier, and then scan it into the computer to be lettered on screen, with a printout at A4 size. Also, artefact illustration remains a task demanding traditional artistic ability, although optical and mechanical pantographs have long been in use and there are now digital shortcuts. Decorated potsherds, for instance, can be scanned into a computer and a line drawing built up on the resulting image or the image itself used without modification. However, perhaps the line illustration of flaked stone artefacts remains a task best tackled with ink and paper. The act of drawing involves an interpretation of flaking details that a scanned image or a high-resolution photograph might not provide. Such drawings require a specialized skill mastered by relatively few (Mumford 1983), so that poor-quality published examples still appear all too often.

Whether line drawings are done by digital or traditional methods, their production raises other important issues that the archaeologist must consider. Any drawing is shaped by the artist's perception. It is an old idea that a good way to understand something is to draw it, but the artist must also have the capacity to convey that understanding to the person using the illustration, who has not seen the subject that has been depicted. A conventional visual 'language' has developed that attempts to fulfil this requirement, involving systematic shading, stippling, variations in line thickness and a variety of symbols such as those used on archaeological section drawings. Other conventions have also been generally adopted; for example, the practice of drawing pots so that one half shows the exterior surface and the other half shows the pot wall in section and part of the pot's interior. If a drawing is to get its intended message across to the user, matters such as these need careful attention. In addition, the overall composition and design of a drawing can be of major importance for its impact on the user. The accuracy of the drawing is also important, although the scale of representation of the original subject needs to be remembered. The thickness of a line on a published small-scale site plan might represent as much as 50 centimetres on the ground, making field measurements to the nearest centimetre pointless. Accuracy is thus a relative matter, particularly given the published size of many archaeological drawings even on an A4 page, let alone the smaller formats that archaeologists are often required to use.

Copyright permissions

One advantage to preparing one's own photographs or drawings for publication is that usually one owns the copyright, although some journals and book publishers ask the author to surrender copyright while retaining the right to republish illustrations elsewhere. On many occasions, however, archaeological authors will need to publish illustrations that have been done by other archaeologists and in most cases already published elsewhere. This is particularly the case for writers of synthetic works and textbooks, especially those intended for a general readership. In all such instances the author will have to seek the permission of the copyright holder before using an illustration. This can be a time-consuming task involving correspondence with authors, photographers, artists, editors or publishers, seeking the necessary approval. E-mail helps in this process, but replies are often slow to arrive and sometimes they merely say that the copyright is actually owned by someone else whose identity might not be known to one's correspondent. In some cases there is no reply to repeated requests; in others it proves impossible to discover who owns the copyright because a journal or a publisher no longer exists or the original photographer or artist is dead. This whole exercise can also be costly for an author. Generally, professional colleagues will grant permission free of charge, subject of course to a published acknowledgement of the source of an illustration (and have a right to expect similar treatment in return), but some publishers, major museums, libraries and other institutions might demand a substantial fee before giving permission. For someone writing a major general text, this can be a real problem; academic authors gain little profit from book royalties (where these are offered) as it is; if they also have to bear the cost of copyright clearances they might sustain a loss. Without doubt this situation is getting worse, and copyright permissions are a matter to which archaeological authors must give careful attention. In addition, they need to be aware that illustrations downloaded from the Internet might also need clearance from the copyright holder before they can be published. As well as the necessary permission, a good copy of the original illustration will be needed, although a scan of the previously published version is often usable with only marginal loss of quality. Acquiring such a copy can again add to the author's expenses. In the late 1950s, when Gordon Childe's books were sold after his death, it was rumoured that some of their pages had holes in them where he had simply cut out illustrations that he needed for his own publications. The poor quality of some published results suggests that it might have been true; it is not a method to be recommended.

Integrating text and illustrations

Having prepared or otherwise obtained the illustrations that one needs, the next thing to consider is how to use them. This is a matter to which the archaeological author needs to give very great attention indeed. At the one extreme, it seems that some writers only bother about illustrations after they have already completed their text. At the other extreme is the notion that it is desirable to prepare the illustrations before writing the text. The former strategy can result in a weak relationship between illustrations and text; the latter can waste time preparing illustrations that are eventually found to be unnecessary or even irrelevant and are therefore not used. The best way is to decide on illustrations as one writes, leaving their individual preparation or acquisition until later if necessary but making a careful list of what is needed as one proceeds. By this means it is possible to achieve a close integration of text and picture, so that each explains the other and strengthens communication with the reader. A common failure in this respect is the way maps are used in some archaeological publications. When reading a text, how often does one find the name of a site, or place, or river or other feature that does not appear on the relevant map? This results from a failure to realize that before drawing such a map, one should list the items that need to be included on it as one writes the text, so that there is a direct relationship between the text and the map. This can also apply to more general matters such as the area represented on the map, the presence of high ground, differences in vegetation, rainfall distribution and so on. In passing, it should be recollected that every map should have a bar scale, not a fractional scale, should have an indication of the direction of north or give the latitude and longitude, and should include an inset map at a much smaller scale showing the location, in the relevant continent or country, of the area shown in the main map. The integration of text and illustration will be most easily achieved if one has an actual copy of the intended illustration, or at least a draft of it, in front of one as one writes.

Illustrations need captions, and caption writing is an art in itself. It needs to be done while looking closely at both the illustration and the relevant text, so that any necessary explanation is provided but repetition or contradiction avoided. Captions unduly repetitious of text are all too common and verbose overlong captions even more so. It is quite unnecessary to say, 'Photograph of . . . ' or 'Map of . . . ', in cases where the character of the illustration is clearly apparent, and captions that state the obvious in other ways are to be avoided. Generally, editors and publishers dislike lengthy captions (although there are exceptions), and I like to keep mine to two or three lines wherever possible. The most difficult in this respect are those that have to include a numbered list of sites or artefacts. Otherwise it is remarkable how many words can be trimmed off one's captions to make them more concise and direct. I prefer to have captions set in a different font from the text, such as italic, and to be placed beneath the illustration spaced away from the nearest line of text, but such matters are of course usually determined by the 'house style' of the publication or publisher, and the position of the caption relative to the illustration can vary.

Numbering the illustrations is another matter to which an author should give early attention, preferably in the course of writing the text. For books a common practice now is to number illustrations within each chapter, so that, for example, 'Fig. 4.8' is the eighth illustration in the fourth chapter (the choice of 'Fig.' or 'Figure' usually depends on the publisher). The great advantage of this method is that, if an illustration is added or removed at some stage after the initial numbering, it is only necessary to renumber the illustrations in one chapter and not those in a large part of the book. However, for journal papers and other articles, the method of numbering will have to conform to the style of the publication. In my own case I also prefer to keep the numbering of illustrations as simple as possible; I call them all 'figures' whether they are photographs, drawings, maps, histograms or whatever. The only exceptions are tables, which technically are not illustrations at all but part of the text (although usually supplied to a publisher on sheets separate from the text). Tables carry their caption within their layout, usually at the top, each being labelled 'Table 1', 'Table 2' and so on. In books they might be numbered separately within each chapter, as mentioned earlier in the case of figures.

Except for the most popular publications, the archaeological author will want to include references within the text to each of the illustrations and tables. This is usually done by inserting the appropriate reference within brackets as one writes; for example, '(Fig. 3.2)' or '(Table 5.1)' in a book, and appropriate equivalents in a journal paper. There might also be occasions when direct discussion of an illustration or table will necessitate the inclusion of such references without brackets, such as 'As can be seen in Figure 3.2 ...' It should be noted that, although in such cases the word 'Figure' will be given in full, in references within brackets it is often abbreviated and the word 'see' is not needed. However, all such practices can vary depending on the requirements of editors or publishers. The reason that such in-text referencing to figures and tables is so important is that it helps to integrate such material with the text. By this means the reader is repeatedly reminded to look at the relevant illustration at the point in the text where it will be most helpful. This, of course, raises the problem of positioning the figures and tables; in each case they will need to be in the same numerical order as the in-text references and as near as possible to that reference. Their order will be determined by the first time that each is referred to, so that for example a subsequent reference to Figure 1 might occur at any point later in the sequence.

Information for the editor or publisher

The real difficulty, as anyone will realize who has ever attempted a book layout, is that quite often it is physically impossible to position a particular illustration near to the point in the text where it is first referred to. A large number of illustrations in proportion to a relatively modest amount of text, or the necessity to find a full page for a particular illustration, can result in a figure or table being several pages away from the point in the text where it is needed. Publishers usually employ experts at book design and layout who can solve some of these problems, but they cannot work miracles and it is wise for the author to provide them with two helpful pieces of information. One is to enter hand-written notes between two horizontal lines in the left margin of the typescript, adjacent to each first in-text reference, such as 'Fig. 6.7 about here'. This will tell the layout person that you want that particular item as close as possible to that point. There might also be special cases that need to be indicated, such as 'Figs. 6.8 & 6.9 must be on facing pages about here'. The second piece of information that should be provided is some guidance about illustration size. In my first book many years ago, drawings of ground-stone axes were printed unnecessarily large but vital excavated sections were too small, and in the end the fault was mine, not the publisher's. It is wise to write on the back of hard copies or include some direction with digital material, advising on desired sizes, such as 'This plan should have a whole page', or 'This map will require landscaping' (i.e., printing on the page long-ways), or 'This graph needs a half-page.' One might even try indicating reduction factors, such as 'This drawing is designed for reduction to 75%', but instructions of a more general nature are probably enough and less likely to alienate the layout specialist!

Even when all the figures and tables are in digital form, many editors and publishers also require a set of hard copies as well. It is wise to mark these in the manner that was common in the pre-digital age, writing an identification in soft pencil on their backs, such as 'Miller Fig. 5.9', and indicating the direction of the top of the illustration with an arrow and the word 'Top' (although this is not necessary for tables). Some printers are quite capable of printing an illustration upside-down, particularly if it consists of line work without lettering or numerals or is a photograph of something unfamiliar to them. Vertical aerial photographs are particularly at risk of this; by convention they are always printed with the north at the top, but the printer will have no means of knowing the correct orientation unless the top has been clearly indicated. As for the use of a *soft* pencil for marking the back of hard copies, this is to prevent the front of the drawing or photograph being 'embossed' by the writing on the other side. Such marks might reduce the quality of the image if for some reason the printer decides to scan the hard copy rather than use the digital version. For the same reason it is good practice to protect hard copies from damage by submitting them in separate clear plastic protective covers, each also labelled (on its front) with the author's surname and the number of the figure or table.

The captions for the figures should be listed double-spaced on sheets separate from the text, bearing in mind that, in the case of a book, abbreviated versions of these captions will also be needed for the figures list that will appear at its beginning. All of this might seem a lot of fuss, but however careful an author is, things can still go wrong. In a book that I once edited, the printer apparently lost one of the photographs, then filled the space by repeating a different photograph from another part of the book, putting the caption beneath it that belonged with the missing photograph. Such an obvious mistake could surely be remedied at proof stage one would think, but no, in spite of clear red-ink instructions from myself, this ludicrous error still appeared in the published book.

Quantity and quality of illustrations

It is often difficult for an author to decide on the number of illustrations (and tables) to be included in a text. Often the editor or publisher, in the latter case usually as one of the terms of a contract, will determine this number. In many cases an author will want to include more than the stipulated number, which will frequently be specified as so many photographs and so many line drawings, with any colour illustrations needing special justification. As mentioned in Chapter 3, disagreement on the quantity and character of visual material can easily become a cause of friction between author and editor or publisher, and this should be avoided if possible. In most cases, the archaeological author must try to keep within the guidelines set out by a publisher or forming part of a journal policy. This can result in some tough decision making; many things that I have written started off with more illustrations and tables than were eventually included when I submitted the book or paper for publication. The crucial question to ask oneself is what the particular illustration or table is actually doing to get the message of the text across to the reader. For example, a paper discussing an excavation will need a map of the site's locality, a plan of the excavated features and a section drawing or drawings of the principal stratification, but photographs of each excavated cutting might be unnecessary. Drawings or photographs of artefacts will also be needed but ought to be representative rather than comprehensive; there might be little point in illustrating every piece of broken pottery. Thus the amount of visual material that is necessary will often be apparent from the purpose of the text that it has to support. In turn, that purpose will be determined not only by the research objective in the case of scholarly writing but also by the intended readership in all writing. Thus a specialized paper discussing a particular artefact might only need one or two black-and-white photographs, but a glossy popular book about a large excavation might require a hundred or more illustrations, many of them in colour. It is all a matter of deciding what is appropriate for the text in question; a wisely chosen picture might even replace a turgid paragraph.

If quantity is sometimes a problem, quality is perhaps more frequently so. Even after some decades of professionalized and intellectualized archaeology, I still see publications in which the maps need a magnifying glass and the photographs look like a wet night in the city. Considering the improvements in technology for both producing and printing illustrations, it is remarkable that some archaeological publications even now include the sort of visual material that Mortimer Wheeler parodied over a half-century ago, when he reprinted a photograph that consisted of a black splodge labelled 'Sir Flinders Petrie in the courtyard of the School in Jerusalem' (Wheeler 1954: Plate XXIA). Black splodges remain popular with archaeologists, but more common are excavation photographs of sites in sunnier parts of the world that have dense shadow obscuring part of the subject. Far more effort is needed to prevent this problem by taking such photographs during cloudy or hazy conditions, or by breaking up the shadows with reflected light or with flash or by 'splitting' the exposure. Other common weaknesses amongst published excavation photographs have already been mentioned earlier in this chapter, but there is also the tendency to leave equipment lying about in the view, to include oversized scruffy identification boards and to fail to remove layout strings.

In addition, although the presence of a human figure in a photograph can provide both a scale and a little human interest, both the choice of person and their positioning need careful thought. An informed perusal of the archaeological literature suggests that several generations of long-suffering wives, husbands, lovers and others have been prevailed upon to act as human ranging rods and not always with the happiest results. My favourite is a published photograph where the human scale has been positioned without sufficient consideration of the background, with the result that a healthy tree appears to be growing out of the head of the unfortunate person.

One could go on and on in this vein but it is all too easy to criticize, and most of us have at some time published photographs that were unsatisfactory in one way or another, including artefact and other archaeological photography as well as the excavation and fieldwork photography discussed earlier. Instead, it is more helpful to consider a selection of archaeological photographs that do communicate a clear 'message' to the reader and demonstrate the high quality that can be obtained with skill and care (Figs. 1–16). Details of these photographs are given in the relevant captions. In this book I am restricted to black-and-white photographs, but recent issues of the journal *Antiquity* have contained some good examples of archaeological photographs in colour, following each editorial, to which the reader should refer. The editor, Martin Carver, initiated this practice with the remark that 'the modern archaeologist does not know how to point a camera' because 'we have given up composing'. He wondered how to 'encourage the archaeological world to enhance its pictures – pictures on which the health and fame of our subject so depends' and so invited people to send in their finest photographs from which a selection could be included in each issue of his journal (Carver 2006: 517–518). The results have been impressive and are worth thoughtful consideration.

However, for reasons already discussed, line drawings have tended to be a more numerous form of archaeological illustration than photographs, although with improvements in printing technology this is less so than in the past. Nevertheless, the most common failure with published drawings remains overreduction, sometimes the fault of publishers or editors but often because the archaeological artist has not given sufficient thought to line thickness, lettering size, shading density or aspect ratio. Here again, rather than criticizing, it is more useful to consider a small number of good examples of relevant illustrations (Figs. 17–29). As with the photographs, the chosen drawings are discussed in each caption. So far as possible, these figures provide a representative series of the sort of drawings common in archaeological publications. Although the method employed to produce each of them is sometimes uncertain, they seem to be mainly hand drawn with few computer-drawn examples. Early digital artwork was sometimes of inferior quality and even now lack of expertise can produce poor drawings, but the future clearly lies with computer graphics. Nevertheless, whether one operates with pen or keyboard, archaeological draughtsmanship still requires skill and careful thought.

Conclusion

The choice of the photographs and drawings shown in the figures in this chapter is as objective as I could make it, within the constraints of copyright clearance. The main criterion influencing my choice has been that the pictures 'should talk', as suggested in the title of the chapter; indeed at the beginning of each caption I have tried to indicate what the illustration 'says' to me. However, there is inevitably subjectivity involved, and each reader might have chosen differently because different people 'read' images in different ways. This is particularly the case with people from different cultural backgrounds. Therefore, I invite each one of you to attempt your own choice from the enormous range of existing archaeological literature. Merely attempting to make such a choice makes one question what qualities define a good archaeological photograph or drawing, and such questioning might make all of us try to improve our own work. Yet, in addition to photographs and drawings, there is another type of 'illustration' that has been touched on but not explored in this chapter, that of archaeological tables (Figs. 30 & 31). This is because they are often treated as part of the text rather than as true illustrations. As such their consideration belongs more properly in the next chapter, which considers the process of writing for different types of archaeological publication. In the meantime, it is important to conclude this chapter by reiterating the point made at its beginning: that pictures are extremely important in nearly all archaeological writing. Many years ago when I was a student of archaeology, Grahame Clark told a group of us to go away and look at a particular paper that he regarded as important. There was a brief silence and then someone remarked, 'But sir, it's in Polish!' The response was immediate: 'That's alright; the pictures are in English.'

Figure 1. Eloquent landscape. Oblique aerial photograph of the deserted medieval village of North Marefield, Leicestershire, England, 1965. Photograph by J. K. St Joseph (St Joseph 1967: Plate XXIV). Courtesy of Antiquity Publications.

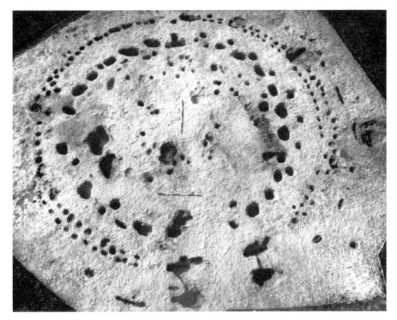

Figure 2. Elevated explanation. An excavated Iron Age house on Pimperne Down, Dorset, England, 1962. Photograph by I. M. Blake from a height of 65 feet (20 metres) (Harding and Blake 1963: Plate VIII). Scale of 6 feet (1.8 metres). Courtesy of Antiquity Publications, I. M. Blake and D. W. Harding.

Figure 3. Investigating structure. An excavated section through a ditch and rampart at Danebury Iron Age hill fort, Hampshire, England, 1969. Photograph by D. Leigh (Cunliffe 1971: Plate XLI). Copyright reserved, Society of Antiquaries of London.

Figure 4. Unusual survivor. Excavated hurdle track dated to about 3000 BC, Walton Heath, Somerset, England. Photograph by John Coles for Somerset Levels Project 1975 (Coles and Orme 1976: Plate VIII). Scale of 1 metre. Courtesy of Antiquity Publications and the photographer.

Figure 5. Ghost ship. Excavating the Sutton Hoo burial ship, dating to the seventh century AD, Suffolk, England, 1965–1967. Photograph by Peter M. Warren (Bruce-Mitford 1968: Frontispiece). Courtesy of Antiquity Publications.

Figure 6. United in death. Excavated burial of an adult and two children, dating to the seventh millennium BC, at Nea Nikomedeia, Greek Macedonia, 1961 (Rodden 1962: Plate XLII). Scale in inches and centimetres. Reproduced by permission of the Prehistoric Society.

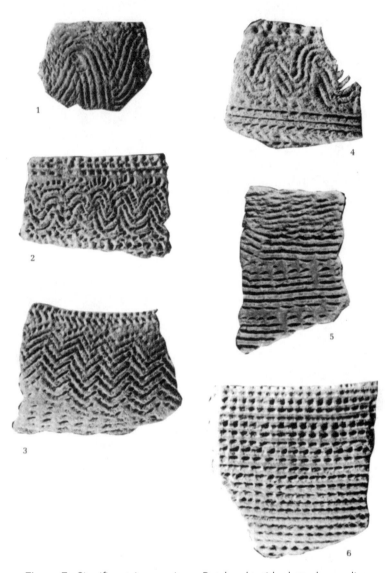

Figure 7. Significant impressions. Potsherds with dotted wavy-line patterns from Jebel Moya, Sudan, dating to the fifth millennium BC (Caneva 1991: Figure 3). Original lacks a scale. Courtesy of Antiquity Publications and the author.

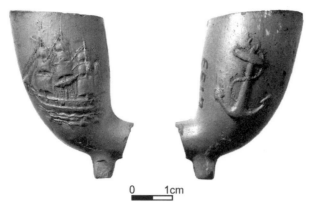

0   1cm

Figure 8. Remembering the voyage out. Two sides of the bowl of a nineteenth-century clay smoking pipe, excavated at Lake Innes Estate, Port Macquarie, New South Wales. Photograph by Rudy Frank (Connah 2007: Figure 10.7–3).

Figure 9. Documenting beliefs. Detail on a silver bowl from Gundestrup, Denmark, dating to the first century BC. Photograph by Larsen (Klindt-Jensen 1959: Plate XVII). Height 210 millimetres. Courtesy of Antiquity Publications.

Figure 10. Evidence of skill. Scanning electron micrograph of granulation on a gold necklace torc, dating to the first century BC, from near Winchester, England. The diameter of each granule is about 2 millimetres. Photograph by Susan La Niece (Hill et al. 2004: Figure 8a). Copyright reserved, Society of Antiquaries of London.

Figure 11. Face from the past. Wooden sculpture of the head of a man with one eye, from Gallo-Roman Auvergne, France, height 38 centimetres. Photograph by Levasseur, Clermont-Ferrand (Vatin 1972: Plate VI). Courtesy of Antiquity Publications.

Figure 12. History in stone. Cormac's Chapel, Cashel, Co. Tipperary, Ireland, dating to the twelfth century AD. Photograph by Malcolm Thurlby (Hunt 2004: Figure 9). Reproduced courtesy of the Society of Antiquaries of London and the photographer.

Figure 13. Expression of faith. Stone carving of an unknown saint, from Congresbury, Somerset, England, dating to the eleventh century AD, height about 80 centimetres (Oakes and Costen 2003: Figure 7). Copyright reserved, Society of Antiquaries of London. Reproduced courtesy of the authors.

Figure 14. Craftsman's legacy. Detail of the hammerbeam roof of the Pilgrims' Hall, Winchester, England, dating to the fourteenth century AD (Crook 1991: Plate XLIIa). Reproduced courtesy of the Society of Antiquaries of London. © Dr John Crook FSA.

Figure 15. Forgotten tragedy. Remains of the Dutch East Indiaman *Amsterdam*, wrecked near Hastings, England, in 1749. Photograph by Peter Marsden (Marsden 1972: Plate XXV). Courtesy of Antiquity Publications and the photographer.

Figure 16. Recapturing the past. Conservation in progress at Stone-henge in 1958 (Daniel 1959: Frontispiece). Courtesy of Antiquity Publications.

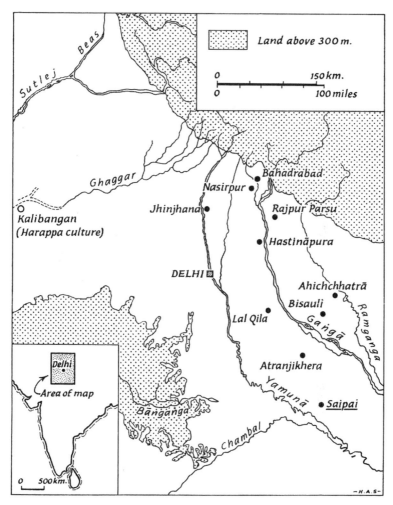

Figure 17. Geographical clarity. Map by H. A. Shelley, drawn for *Antiquity* (Lal 1972: Figure 1). Courtesy of Antiquity Publications.

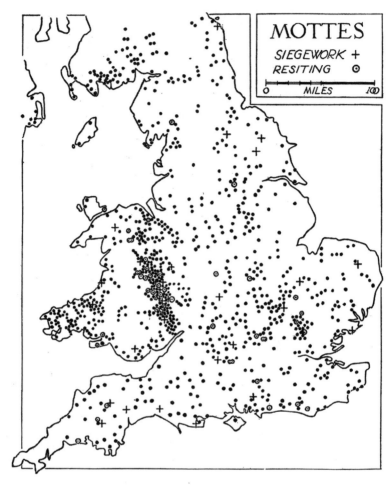

Figure 18. Pattern of insecurity. Distribution of mottes (medieval castle mounds) in England, Wales, and southern Scotland (Renn 1959: Figure 3). Courtesy of Antiquity Publications and the author.

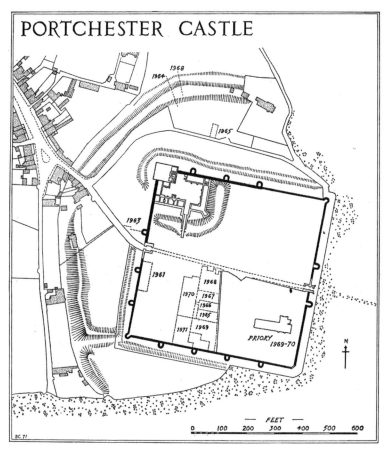

Figure 19. Organized defence. Plan of Portchester Castle, Hampshire, England, showing locations of excavations (Cunliffe 1972: Figure 1). Copyright reserved, Society of Antiquaries of London.

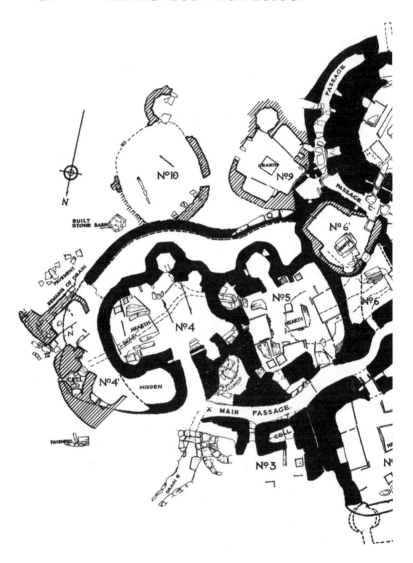

Figure 20. Cold comfort. Plan of excavated village at Skara Brae, Orkney, dating to the third millennium BC (Childe 1931: facing p.48). Courtesy of Antiquity Publications.

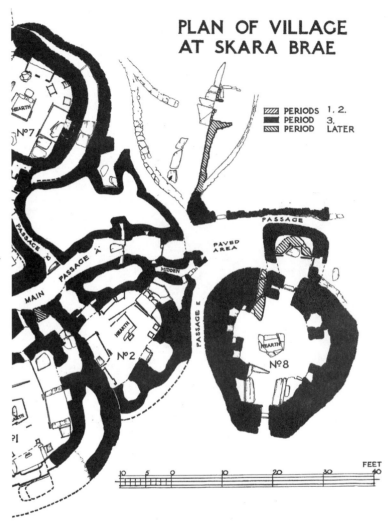

PLAN OF VILLAGE
AT SKARA BRAE

By permission of H.M. Office of Works

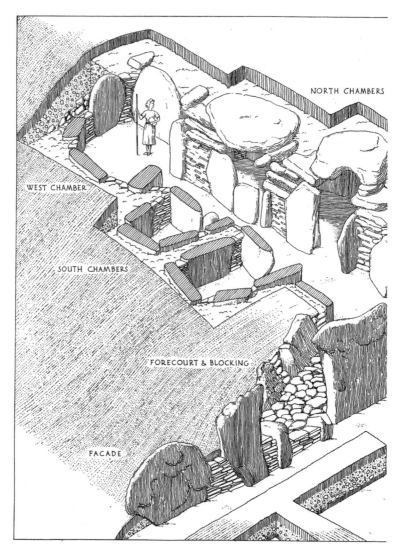

NORTH CHAMBERS

WEST CHAMBER

SOUTH CHAMBERS

FORECOURT & BLOCKING

FACADE

Figure 21. Housing the dead. Isometric drawing of West Kennet Long Barrow, Wiltshire, England, dating to the fourth millennium BC. Drawn by Stuart Piggott (Piggott 1958: facing p. 236). Courtesy of Antiquity Publications.

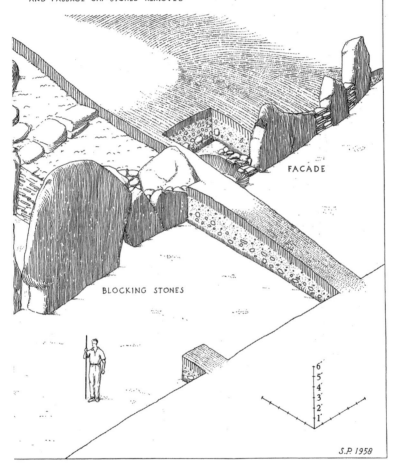

WEST KENNET LONG BARROW

ISOMETRIC VIEW FROM SOUTH-EAST
THE SOUTHERN CHAMBERS SHOWN AS IF CUT AT 3 FT ABOVE FLOOR LEVEL
AND PASSAGE CAP-STONES REMOVED

FACADE

BLOCKING STONES

S.P. 1958

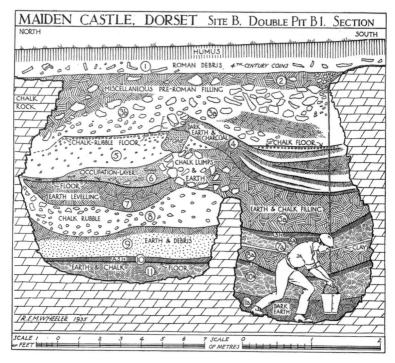

Figure 22. Artistic stratigraphy. Section drawing of Iron Age pit at Maiden Castle, Dorset, England. Drawn by Mortimer Wheeler (Wheeler 1943: Figure 12A). Copyright reserved, Society of Antiquaries of London.

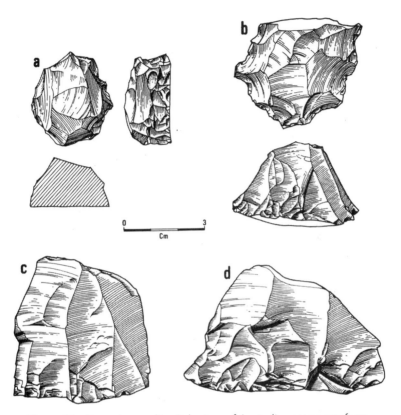

Figure 23. Capturing reality. Selection of Australian stone artefacts. Drawn by Winifred Mumford (White [Schrire] 1971: Figure 12.4). Reproduced by permission of the editors D.J. Mulvaney and J. Golson, the illustrator, and the author.

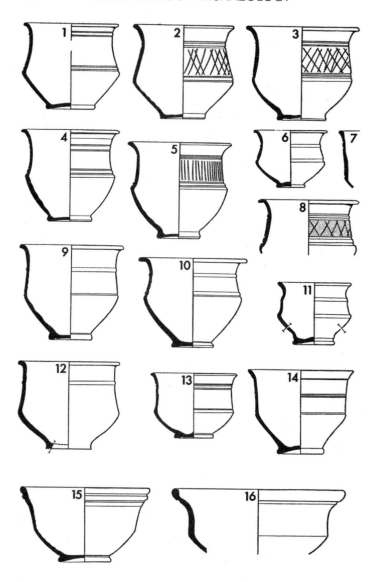

Figure 24. Depicting variability. Roman pots from Little Chester, Derbyshire, England (Brassington 1971: Figure 5). No. 1 is 116 millimetres high. Copyright reserved, Society of Antiquaries of London.

Figure 25. Declaring identity. Reconstruction drawing of the back of a bronze mirror, from Holcombe, Devon, England, dating to the first century AD. Drawn by Philip Compton (Fox 1972: Figure 2). Width 260 millimetres. Courtesy of Antiquity Publications.

Figure 26. Ethnic cleansing. South African rock painting showing Europeans shooting at Bushmen (Dowson 1993: Figure 1). Scale presumed in centimetres. Courtesy of Antiquity Publications.

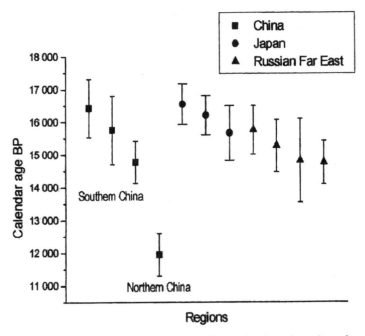

Figure 27. Chronology at a glance. Calibrated radiocarbon dates for the earliest pottery in East Asia (Kuzmin 2006: Figure 2). Courtesy of Antiquity Publications.

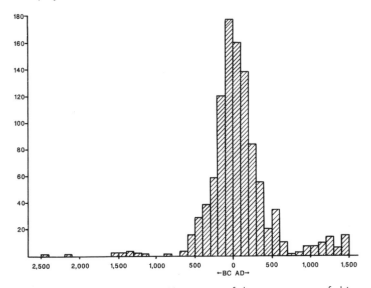

Figure 28. Dangerous times. Histogram of the occurrence of ship-wrecks in the Mediterranean (Parker 1990: Figure 1). Courtesy of Antiquity Publications and the author.

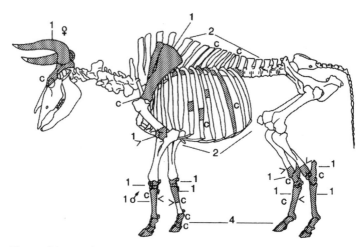

Figure 29. Butchery methods. Recovered skeletal elements of aurochs (hatched) with minimum numbers of individuals for each (group of) element(s) and sex identifications where possible. <: deliberate fractures; C: bones with cutmarks. From Jardinga, Netherlands, dating to the sixth millennium BC (Prummel et al. 2002: Figure 5). Courtesy of Antiquity Publications and the University of Groningen, Groningen Institute of Archaeology.

Species	Jan	Feb	Mar	Apr	May	Jun	Jul	Aug	Sep	Oct	Nov	Dec
Sockeye Salmon						■	■					
Humpback Salmon							■	■				
Chum Salmon								■	■			
Coho Salmon									■	■		
Herring			■	■	■				■	■		
Cod			■	■	■	■						
Halibut			■	■	■	■	■					
Lingcod	■									■	■	■
Rockfish	■				■					■	■	■
Other Bottomfish	■								■	■	■	
Steelhead	■	■	■									
Dolly Varden Char							■	■	■			
Shellfish	■	■								■	■	■
Sea Mammals							■					
Terrestrial Mammals	■	■	■					■	■		■	■

Figure 30. Menu for the year. Table showing seasonal availability of resources in Tebenkof Bay, southeast Alaska (Maschner 1991: Table 1). Courtesy of Antiquity Publications and the author.

Site	Culture	Floor of bark/branches	Wall stakes/posts/tent ring	Flint concentration	Hearth/hearths	Systematic patterning	Dwelling pit/lense	Central posts/stakes
Duvensee 13 (1986)	M	X			X	X		
Duvensee 13 (1989)	M	X				X		
Klosterlund 1 E	M			X	X	X		
Barmosen I	M	X			X	X		X
Ulkestrup I	M	X	X	X	X	X		X
Ulkestrup II	M	X	X	X	X	X		X
Duvensee 6	M	X			X	X	X	X
Duvensee 8	M	X			X	X	X	X
Duvensee 13 (1985)	M	X			X	X	X	X
Hytteberga nr.9	K?	X						X
Hjemsted	M			X	X	X	?	X
Deepcar	M			X	X	X	X	X
Lollikhuse	E			X	X	X		X
Nivå 10	E			X	X	X	X	X
Ageröd I:HC	M/K			X	X	?		X
Rude Mark	M			X	X	X		X
Klosterlund 1W	M			X	X	X		X
Stallerupholm	M			X	X	?		X
Vængesø	M			X	X	X		X
Tobisborg 1:1975	M			X				X
Tobisborg 2:1975	M			X				X
Tobisborg 3:1975	M			X				X
Hagestad 6:2A,1	M			X	?	?		X
Hagestad 6:2A,2	M			X	X			X
Hagestad 6:2A,3	M			X	X	X		X
Hagestad 6:2A,4	M			X				X
Hagestad 44:8A	M			X				X
Møllegabet II	E	X	X	X	X	X	X	X
Bredasten	E			X	X	X	X	X
Leksand I	K/E			X	X			X
Leksand II	K/E			X	X			X
Svanemosen 28	M			X	X	X	X	?
Flaadet	M			X	X	X		X
Saxtorp nr.11	K			X	X		X	X
Skateholm I	E			X	X		X	X
Tågerup 1	E		X	X	X		X	X
Tågerup 2	E			X	X		X	X
Tågerup 'W'	E		X	X				X

Figure 31. Statement of relationships. Table listing Mesolithic dwelling places in south Scandinavia and the features observed in them. M: Maglemose Culture; K: Kongemose Culture; E: Ertebølle Culture (Grøn 2003: Figure 9). Courtesy of Antiquity Publications.

Seven

Pleasing everyone

Writing for different types of publication

One of the principal difficulties concerning archaeological authorship is that it can take such a variety of forms. Chapter 3 examined this subject in terms of the intended readership, and Chapter 5 considered the process of writing in general terms. Now it is necessary to look more closely at how the demands of archaeological writing can vary depending on the type of publication and to consider some of the specific problems that can be encountered in writing for different outlets. In practice, many archaeologists will tend to concentrate on writing for particular types of publication, most commonly for academic journals. Some, however, will range more widely and will write research monographs, scholarly syntheses, textbooks or other works. There will even be those who will spend more time editing the writing of other archaeologists than doing their own. Although satirized by Paul Bahn as a 'crafty way to get your name on the front of a book' (Bahn 1989: 36), such editing also makes important contributions to archaeological publication and has its own difficulties. However, in this chapter attention will be focussed on those forms of writing that most archaeologists might tackle at one time or another: the excavation monograph, the journal paper, the general synthesis and the so-called popular book.

Writing excavation monographs: The curse of the catalogue

It seems appropriate to start with one of the oldest forms of archaeological publication, the research monograph. The principal problem encountered by the writer of this sort of publication is the necessity to present a massive amount of data without merely producing an unreadable catalogue. As in most archaeological writing, there is the difficult task of presenting material evidence on the printed page; things and their patterning in space and time have to be translated into words, illustrations and tables. This task can prove particularly demanding in the case of research monographs, of which the classic excavation report is the most obvious example. This sort of publication can degenerate into a series of lists of artefacts and other data, within a text loaded with information on stratification, typology, faunal analysis, radiocarbon recalibration, statistical methodology and so on. There might also be heavy illustration, in the form of both copious drawings and photographs, some of the latter perhaps in colour. In addition, tables often proliferate, including large and complex examples. Some of the drawings and tables might be so large that 'foldouts' become necessary, in order to avoid overreduction. As if all this is not bad enough, the unfortunate writer will often have to marshal a disparate collection of separate 'reports' by specialists who have examined parts of the excavated evidence, such as geologists, chemists, metallurgists, botanists, palaeoanthropologists, art historians and so on. As a result, in some instances, the archaeological writer will begin to wonder whether she or he is really the author of the resulting book or merely its editor. Indeed, the archaeologist who produces such an excavation monograph is not so much writing a book as producing a work of reference. The result is often a large and expensive publication, sometimes of more than one volume.

It is important to consider why this sort of publication is ever written at all. The shelves of archaeological libraries have many examples of excavation monographs, which in some cases have been rarely read since they were published long ago. I still remember the disappointment of my own first foray into this type of writing; my book *The archaeology of Benin* (Connah 1975) took seven years, off and on, from the start of writing to publication, but was scarcely noticed by archaeological readers when it appeared. So why bother to write such white elephants? The practice seems to have arisen from a traditional conviction amongst archaeologists that the excavated data must be presented in as much detail as possible and should be clearly separated from the often-brief interpretation based on it. It is as if the excavator is attempting to preserve the minutiae of the evidence as a compensation for having destroyed all or part of the site, in the course of obtaining that evidence. Archaeologists of my generation constantly had the fearsome words of R. J. C. Atkinson ringing in their ears:

> The importance of publishing proper reports of archaeological research, and especially of excavations, cannot be too strongly emphasized. For, as has already been said, the excavation of a site involves its destruction; once excavated, the evidence cannot be reconstituted except from the records made by the excavator. Failure to publish these records, therefore, is as much a crime against science as the deliberate suppression of a newly discovered historical document. (Atkinson 1953: 173)

Atkinson was writing about the publication of excavation reports in journals as well as in monographs, but archaeologists have generally agreed that a large excavation needed a large publication to present its results. In this idea, they were reflecting the nineteenth-century tradition of the *magnum opus*, the large and important work that established a scholar's reputation. The inevitable question is, are such publications still relevant in the twenty-first century?

There has, indeed, been a growing uncertainty in recent years about the necessity for this sort of publication, given the time and money that its preparation can require. In Britain, the United States and in some other countries, there has been an enormous growth in archaeological fieldwork, particularly excavation, in the last few decades. Commercial consultants on behalf of developers or heritage agencies have undertaken most of this work, and its results have tended to become buried in unpublished reports. It would probably be impossible to publish all this material in traditional monographs even if there was a wish to do so. Nevertheless, publication remains a matter of concern (Jones et al. 2001). In the opinion of some archaeologists, such detailed evidence is now most efficiently and economically published on the Internet, although the problems of digital archiving and future accessibility are matters of concern (see Chapter 1). Digital data bases devoted to archaeology, such as the Archaeology Data Service and the OASIS project in Britain (ADS 2008; OASIS 2008), are developing powerful tools that can make huge amounts of information available. As early as 1997 the journal *Antiquity* devoted fifty-one pages to a review of electronic archaeology and its potential (Champion and Chippindale 1997). It remains the case, however, that somebody still has to write the material that goes into a digital archive, except where the archive consists of only digitized records. Thus, whether the excavation monograph appears on paper or in a digital form, the archaeological author still has to face the same problem of presenting a mass of complex data in a coherent and readable fashion so that it is available for future users.

The main value of an excavation monograph is as a source of information for future researchers. Therefore, the first consideration for its author is that it should be as easy to use as possible. This means good organization; the field and laboratory records on which the writing is to be based need to be put in the best attainable order before writing commences. That can take some time because even a modest-sized excavation can result in several thousand photographs, large numbers of drawings and many context sheets and other written or computerized records. The time is well spent, however, because disorganized data can adversely affect the structure and content of the monograph, as well as causing interruptions to the writing. Once the raw material has been put in good order, the next task for the writer is to decide which data are to be included and which are to be excluded. Some people have great difficulty with this task and try to include 'everything': a sort of vacuum-cleaner approach that attempts to ensure that nothing is left out. Others compress material so much that the reader is unable to find the crucial detailed evidence for some of the interpretation. What matters most in making decisions about what to include is relevance: do the chosen data contribute to the argument or arguments being presented; do they help to confirm or challenge the hypothesis or hypotheses being assessed? If the answer to this test is negative, then the material in question is probably of descriptive value only, although it might still merit inclusion. If that is the case, care will still be needed to avoid lengthy digressions, and the presentation of information in précis form will sometimes be necessary.

Nevertheless, even if great care is taken with the selection of data for inclusion, the volume of chosen information can still be intimidating. In the case of the text, there are several strategies that can minimize this problem. One is to present as much information as possible in the form of photographs, drawings, diagrams and tables. In my own case, for instance, I like the histogram as an economical and efficient way of presenting numerical variables. However, the benefits of visual material will be squandered if the text still presents information that reasonably alert readers can see for themselves in the illustrations. This sort of repetition does happen and in some cases is made even worse by lengthy illustration captions that say it all yet again. However, the cure can occasionally be worse than the disease; the illustrations might help to reduce the size of the text, but unless great care is taken their numbers can also become excessive. Most writers will find it necessary to be highly selective of the visual and tabulated material; pictures can be repetitive as well as text.

Another strategy that can reduce the length of a monograph is to print the more detailed descriptions in blocks, or even whole pages, of smaller type. This has the advantage of increasing the number of words on a page, as well as helping the reader to skip details that might not be of interest while still reading the main text. The specialist who might need to examine the details is also assisted by their visual separation from the rest of the text. A related method, before personal computers became so common, was to provide detailed data on microfiche inserted loose in a pocket at the end of the book; at one time this was a favoured innovation (Mytum 1978). At least one leading archaeological journal (PPS 1982–1989) took to doing this, but now, years later, if these records have not been lost in whole or in part, or degraded over time, it is difficult to find a working microfiche reader to enable their use. A better strategy is to remove the details from the text and place them in one or more appendices at the end of the monograph, perhaps also printing them in smaller type. This can be a trap for the unwary, however, and the author must be careful that the appendices do not merely become a ragbag of details that will hardly ever be looked at. The same applies to footnotes and endnotes when used for information other than references. The distinction between scholarship and pedantry can be difficult.

Yet another strategy is to accept that the excavation monograph cannot in itself provide an excavation archive. Instead, the monograph can exclude descriptive details of marginal relevance and merely refer the interested reader to the primary excavation records that have been deposited in the archives of a museum, library, university or other institution. Although some archaeologists have long done this, it is a practice that needs to be adopted more widely (Lyon 1989). There have been cases where such material stored in an archaeologist's house has been destroyed in a fire (e.g., Fagan 1978). There are also probably still instances where valuable excavation records are left to rot in someone's garage or attic, or even taken to the local garbage dump, following the death of the archaeologist whose work produced them. However, digital publication on the Internet, as discussed earlier, can provide a final strategy that will surely become more common as time goes on. A printed hard-copy monograph can include a digital address that gives access to the less important descriptive data or even the complete excavation archive. This would allow the more general reader to peruse an uncluttered printed text, while enabling the specialist to investigate the details electronically. Perhaps better still, the entire excavation monograph could be published in a digital form with links that the specialist could open up at will, when the more detailed information or the excavation archive needs to be examined. Nevertheless, the task of the initial writing will remain a challenge, and it is to be hoped that the elasticity of the Internet will not encourage a lack of the organizational and stylistic economy necessary in such writing. Furthermore, unless all the records made during an excavation are to be digital from the beginning, there might still be a need to preserve some original drawings and other hard-copy materials in an appropriate archive. In addition, the enthusiast for digital publication would do well to remember those microfiche from the1980s: is there sufficient permanence in the Internet for the publication of excavation monographs or are we in danger of letting history repeat itself? In the long term, many Web sites could prove ephemeral, and it appears that at the present time long-term digital preservation remains a matter of concern (Brown 2006; Masanès 2006).

Before leaving the subject of writing excavation monographs, there is one more aspect to consider: how to *structure* the text and its contained illustrations and tables. As in more general monographs, chapters can be adopted as the major divisions, and almost certainly subdivisions will also be needed. However, unless care is taken with the latter, there is a danger that they will confuse rather than assist the reader. If the author is writing a monograph to be handled by a publisher, in either hardcopy or digital form, a formal house style might be required in the submitted text, stipulating a particular heading/subheading hierarchy. Otherwise, it is helpful to examine a selection of published excavation monographs to see how different authors have divided and subdivided their work. So far as possible, I favour simplicity in such matters. For example, the hierarchy that I used in the text of a recent excavation monograph (Connah 2007) was as follows. The most important division was the chapter, with its number and title centred at the top of a recto (right-hand) page. They were in a larger type (Times 16 point) than the main body of the text (Times 12 point) and in bold. Next was a subheading aligned with the left-hand margin, in smaller type (Times 14 point) than the chapter heading but still larger than the main body of the text and in bold. Third was a subheading also aligned with the left-hand margin, in smaller type (Times 12 point) than the previous subheading but the same size as the main body of the text and in bold. Fourth was again a subheading aligned with the left-hand margin but in bold italic type of the same size as the main body of the text. I tried to avoid further subdivision, but where a fifth one became essential I used an italic subheading aligned with the left-hand margin but in nonbold type of the same size as the main body of the text into which it ran. Although I did not do so in this example, it is also sometimes appropriate to number the sequence of subheadings, using a combination of upper-case Roman numerals, Arabic numerals, lower-case Roman numerals and lower-case letters. Each number or letter should be of the same font and type size as the subheading to which it is attached. However, unless a publisher requires a particular heading hierarchy, authors should adopt one that is most suited to their own text and its illustrations and tables. Having adopted it, they must be rigorously consistent; disorganized subheadings can be very confusing for a reader. It should also be accepted that a publisher's copy editor, or layout and book designer or typographer will most likely change all the fonts and type sizes, including the headings and subheadings. It will therefore be important at the proof stage that the author ensures that the intended hierarchy has been retained in spite of changes in its appearance.

Writing for journals and edited collections: Bread-and-butter work

Almost certainly an archaeologist's first publication will be a paper for an academic journal, or for a collection of papers in an edited monograph or perhaps for the proceedings of a conference to which the writer contributed. Indeed, most of the publications produced by archaeological writers are of these types. If writing a paper for a journal, the archaeologist will have to choose the publication with care, for the reasons already discussed in Chapter 3, although sometimes a journal editor will request a paper from an author and perhaps even specify the subject that is to be written about. However, this is more likely to be the case with an edited collection of papers, where the editor might have very precise ideas about the paper being sought. In contrast, inclusion in the published proceedings of a conference will usually be an almost automatic outcome of having participated in the conference, although some authors might prefer to publish elsewhere and some editors might solicit additional papers from writers who were not present at the conference. It follows that it is advantageous, if not essential, for the archaeologist writing for any of these outlets to know as much as possible about the form that publication will take, before commencing to write.

Having identified the publication for which one is writing, the next step is to obtain a copy of its 'Instructions to contributors'. For journals, these instructions can vary greatly in length and detail. There are very few requirements in some cases; in others they can occupy many pages. One of my 'favourites' is a well-known journal that has thirty-nine pages of extraordinarily detailed instructions. In such cases, the relevant material is often available on the Internet Web page for the journal, rather than being printed at the end of each volume, as was the traditional practice. The purpose of such 'Instructions' is to ensure that a uniform house style for the journal is maintained and that there is consistency even in minor matters of presentation, such as the use of hyphens or italics. In practice, the instructions are there in order to save editors the considerable time that would otherwise be spent in altering disparate texts to attain uniformity. A list of references that is incorrectly presented, for instance, can take many hours to put right. Most editors of archaeological academic journals are other professional archaeologists who are unpaid volunteers doing the work in their 'spare' time. Many archaeological authors will find themselves in this role at some time in their careers; therefore it is important to treat an editor in the manner that one would wish to be treated oneself. However, the reality is that journal editors continually find that writers submit papers without following the instructions carefully enough and occasionally without looking at them at all. The more self-opinionated writers sometimes ignore even statements about maximum length, which varies so much from journal to journal. The archaeologist who fails in this respect has no reason to complain if the paper is promptly returned with a request that it be altered to meet the specified requirements of the journal. Editors of collections of papers or conference proceedings will also usually have their own instructions, with which they expect authors to comply, and in cases where a commercial publisher is involved there will be little tolerance of inattention by contributors.

Once a writer has become familiar with the instructions to contributors for the chosen journal or other edited publication, what then? As a person who has edited as well as written journal and other papers, I am of the opinion that the most important thing is that the intended paper must have something of significance to say. This might sound obvious, but a perusal of many journals and edited collections or proceedings will reveal some papers that are at best inconsequential, at worst pointless. In such cases, the reader is justified in asking, 'So what?' The fault might be the author's, but it can also sometimes be the editor's. Perhaps the editorial process has not been selective enough or a publication deadline had to be met with whatever material was to hand. Somebody once remarked that a journal is like a train standing at a railway station; it has to leave at the scheduled time whether all the seats are full or not. Inevitably, some less desirable passengers might be allowed to board at the last minute. However, having something of significance to say is one thing; knowing how to say it is another. It is vital that the paper be tightly structured around the objective or objectives that the writer has. To achieve this requires economy and precision in introducing the subject or argument, in presenting the relevant data, in explaining its analysis and in advancing an interpretation. Care will be needed with heading and subheading hierarchy and with paragraph and sentence structure, and close attention must be given to clarity of expression and choice of vocabulary. Care will also be needed with the selection of illustrations and tables, having regard to some of the discussion of this subject in Chapter 6. A tight integration of this material with the text is particularly important.

Tables are frequently used in papers for journals and similar outlets; their design merits careful thought and close attention (Chapter 6, Figs. 29 & 30). Large and complex tables can create problems for both editor and printer, quite apart from the difficulty that the eventual reader might have in understanding them. Changes in technology have made tables much easier to reproduce than some years ago, when they had to be hand set, but it is still worth finding the simplest way to present tabulated information. Attention will be needed to the use of horizontal and vertical rules of different thicknesses or of white space to divide rows and columns. Thoughtful use of bold, italic and normal numerals, letters or symbols, to denote quantities or characteristics within the cells of a table, will also be helpful. Care will be needed to distinguish between cell entries that indicate a nil quantity and those that indicate the absence or nonapplicability of a particular measurement. The labelling of rows and columns at the margins of a table also needs to be clear and unambiguous, and it is vital that it be immediately apparent what a table is recording, such as grams, millimetres, numbers of specimens, minimum numbers of animals, etc. It is remarkable how such essential information can be forgotten when creating a table. Finally, every table should be clearly labelled with a table number and a descriptive title that tells the reader what it is about. This title is best put in larger type than the contents of the table and perhaps in bold. Unlike illustration captions, the title of a table is often an integral part of the table design, usually placed at its top so that any explanatory notes that are needed can be put in smaller type below the table. It will be claimed that all these matters can be automatically attended to by the appropriate software, and certainly computers have made life easier than when some larger tables had to be typed on a mechanical typewriter with a (relatively rare) 18-inch (457-mm) carriage. Nevertheless, the preparation of tables still requires careful attention by an author. Not long ago a colleague and I sent a joint paper to a journal editor containing some half-dozen tables, in addition to illustrations. We were subsequently surprised to find that the editor was able to compress our tables into just two tables. The editor had seen possibilities that we had missed, but we should not have missed them.

Archaeological authors not only write papers; they also read papers. In particular they tend to read papers written by others who are in the same general area of the discipline. Some papers will impress them; others might be found inadequate. When reading such papers, it is a useful exercise to sort them into those papers that seem to succeed in their stated intention and those that do this less well or fail to do it at all. A careful examination can often reveal the reasons for such success or lack of it, indicating things that an author might emulate or avoid in her or his own writing. In this way it is possible to learn something from the achievements of some writers and from the failures of others. However, the subject matter of archaeological papers is so diverse, and writers' approaches to different subjects so varied that it is important that the papers by other writers have some comparability to the paper one is writing. With this in mind, it is also worthwhile to read a selection of papers that have been published in recent issues of the journal to which one intends to submit one's own paper. All this might seem obvious, but it is remarkable how often such obvious strategies are overlooked.

One of the principal difficulties when writing a paper is controlling its length, including its illustrations and tables where present. I have always had the impression that many archaeologists tend to be long-winded when they write the text of a paper. Indeed, I have to admit that at one time I was guilty of this and even now at times cannot claim to be without fault. The problem is that we archaeologists always have such a lot of interesting information that we want to mention; we tend to forget that only the information relevant to the purpose of the paper should be included. We also tend to over-illustrate on some occasions. It is not unknown, for instance, for a writer to submit an extra illustration or two in order to surreptitiously provide an editor with material to cut out, thus reducing the risk of a similar fate for the really necessary images. In addition, we have a weakness for including too many tables in our papers. After all, we have all these photographs or drawings or tables that took us so much time to prepare, so surely we must be able to fit them into the paper somewhere. Such an approach risks editorial rejection or at least substantial revision and the removal of material that should not have been included in the first place.

One of my earliest introductions to the discipline of brevity when writing papers occurred many years ago when a radiologist and I collaborated on a paper about the pathology of some human skeletal material that I had excavated in Nigeria. My colleague was the product of a prestigious American medical school, and he warned me from the beginning that medical journals would not tolerate what he saw as the easy-going attitude of archaeological journals regarding paper length. This seemed good advice, so we submitted a modest paper of perhaps 3,000 words, with a not unreasonable number of radiographs and bone-section photographs selected from the more than 300 bones that had been examined. We sent the paper to one of the leading radiology journals in America. Back it came with a polite note saying that it was of interest and that they would like to publish it but it was too long; we should shorten the text and reduce the amount of illustration. From memory, I think we halved the length of the text and reduced the illustrations to six before we sent it off again. Once more it returned; it was still too long, and could we please shorten it some more? We did as requested and it was subsequently published as a paper of about 1,000 words, with our six illustrations grouped into two figures (Bohrer and Connah 1971).

For writers of papers who wish to avoid that sort of experience, a strict economy in text, illustrations and tables is essential. One needs to ask oneself, regarding each of these components, what is *necessary*. However, this is easier said than done, and the relevant journal editor might still judge the finished paper excessive. To avoid this happening, the writer will need to do some tough revising, even if she or he is convinced that the paper already has a concise text and only essential illustrations and tables. This is not easy for a writer; editing one's own material is always difficult. As mentioned at the end of Chapter 5, it helps if one can put the paper away for a while, so that one returns to it without the familiarity that developed during its writing. It really is remarkable what can then be done, if one is able to distance oneself from the paper and read it as if somebody else had written it. Recently I had to tackle the revision of a collaborated paper of a little more than 6,000 words, which was intended for a journal that normally would not publish articles longer than 5,000 words. It had eight illustrations and two tables, one of them quite small, which seemed reasonable. It was the length of the text that was the problem. I spent a day on it and was able to reduce its length to less than 5,400 words, a cut of more than 11 percent that also removed seven entries from the reference list. The result was a much-improved paper but one that might still benefit from further shortening. We hardly ever write anything that could not be written better and more briefly. One of the keys to effective writing is knowing what to leave out.

Sadly, even the most concise and carefully revised paper might only be read by a relatively small number of those who peruse the issue of the journal in which it appears. Far more people will read the abstract provided at its beginning. This literary device, commonly insisted on by the editors of journals and related publications, is probably the most difficult part of the paper to write. Arguably, it is also the most important part of a paper, but it is frequently given inadequate care by writers. It needs to be written after the paper has been written and revised but before submission. The task is difficult because a good abstract is one that *'concentrates in itself the essential information'* [italics in original] of the paper (Landes 1966: 1992). Essentially it is a précis of what the paper has to say, and it is usually of about 150–200 words maximum length. The most common failing in abstract writing is to tell the reader what the paper is about, but not what it contributes. This sort of abstract can be identified by the presence of statements such as 'The type of pottery decoration from the Yau excavation is discussed and its chronology is considered.' What is actually needed is a statement such as 'Pottery excavated from Yau was decorated with roulettes and belonged to the early second millennium AD.' Both of these sentences contain the same number of words, but the second one actually tells the reader something, instead of merely making vague promises. Unfortunately, the writing of abstracts has also suffered from the practice of sending in conference paper abstracts long before a conference takes place, and often before the paper has been written. The outcome can be an abstract that bears little relationship to the paper that is eventually given, but it is the abstract that will be printed in the conference programme and perhaps even published elsewhere, particularly in abstracting journals. Furthermore, just to make the abstract writer's task even more difficult, there is an increasing (and necessary) tendency for journal editors to demand abstracts in French or other languages, as well as in English.

Several other aspects of the gentle art of writing papers also deserve a mention. Referencing and bibliographies have already been considered briefly in Chapter 5, but it is as important to control their length as it is that of the text. Although paper lengths stipulated by journals do not usually include bibliographies, it is nevertheless desirable to avoid elephantine ones that extend over many pages. Experienced editors are usually alert to bibliographies and in-text references that aim to impress rather than to inform. Overreferencing can also result in serious fragmentation of the text, with strings of names, dates and page numbers sometimes continuing for several lines. One book reviewer, for instance, has complained about a text so 'heavily freighted with bibliographic references' that one otherwise short sentence contained thirteen of them (Webster 2007: 1116). This is assuming, of course, that the Harvard System is in use, as appears to be now the case with most archaeological journals. However, there are those who castigate the Harvard System as 'pseudo-science silliness' and prefer 'the civilised use of footnotes' (Kitchen 1998: 627), but the latter archaic system can also balloon out of control, as many a nineteenth-century publication demonstrates.

The point is that referencing, in whatever form it is done (and there are also both endnotes and the Vancouver System), needs to be kept under tight control just like the text.

Another matter to which writers need to give attention is that of consistency in authorship. It will not help bibliographers, readers or other writers if you keep changing what you call yourself. It is no good being John David Jones on one paper but John Jones or John D. Jones or J. D. Jones or J. Jones on other papers. You must decide who you are and stick with it; otherwise your long-suffering colleagues might begin to wonder whether you are just one or several people. Women writers who marry after they have already published under their maiden name have a particular problem with this matter. The more recent practice of retaining their name from before marriage is an obvious solution, but when this is not done, as was commonly the case in the past, a time-honoured strategy has been simply to add the married surname to the surname before marriage, with or without a hyphen. Thus, an invertebrate zoologist that I knew first published under the name Nora Fisher but subsequently under the name Nora Fisher McMillan, a name that she continued to use to the end of her long life, many years after the death of her husband. She had the right idea; it is important to be consistent with authorship.

The writer of a paper will also need to give attention to some other details. It is usually necessary, for instance, to state the author's affiliation after her or his name. Some journals will move this to the bottom of the first page of the paper or even to its end, but it is customary to include it. It should consist of the detailed address of the writer's university department or museum or heritage body or consulting firm or even home. In some cases it might even include an e-mail address, although many writers are understandably wary on that matter. In addition to this statement of affiliation, it is also usual to supply a small number of 'keywords', typically occupying no more than one line and positioned after the abstract. This is to assist in indexing and in the construction and searching of digital data bases. The choice of these words is determined by the subject matter of the paper and needs more careful thought than it is sometimes given. It is as if one is attempting to provide an abstract in ten words or less. Try looking at a selection of published papers by other authors to see how they have represented the content of their papers in their chosen keywords. Finally, the writer of a paper must not forget the acknowledgements section, usually placed at the end of the text, before the reference list. Here one should mention all those who have contributed to the work that led to the writing of the paper or have helped in any significant way. In particular, permissions to reprint illustrations from copyright sources should be mentioned, unless they have been referred to in the individual captions. As with the paper and its list of references, however, the acknowledgements must not be allowed to become too large. Neither should they be allowed to become maudlin; references to one's mum and dad or even to one's pet cat might be tempting but are best avoided!

The foregoing discussion of writing papers for journals has been written with single authorship in mind. I already had something to say about multiple authorship in Chapter 5. Suffice it to add that any form of collaboration in writing needs a more flexible approach than when one writes alone. Working with one other person, or perhaps even two, can be a productive and rewarding experience, particularly if each individual is able to contribute a different perspective and yet is willing to consider an alternative one. Attempting to write a paper with a dozen or more others is another matter. The old joke about an elephant being a horse designed by a committee comes to mind. Similarly, papers written by a committee can finish up in a form that at least some of their co-authors did not intend. One feels that such papers should at least indicate how all the named authors undertook the writing or distinguish clearly those who did the research or other work from the person or persons who also did the actual writing. However, this is enough about writing journal papers. The reader who desires more should perhaps consult an online tutorial on the subject by the University of Colorado libraries (Publish, not perish: The art and craft of publishing in scientific journals).

Seeking the big picture: Writing an archaeological synthesis

Archaeology, by its very nature, is a particularistic subject. We tend to write about individual sites or groups of sites, or types of artefacts, or specific methodologies or selected theories. Increasingly, however, archaeological authors are also writing general syntheses that review a wider subject area, such as an entire region or a whole period in the past or some other general part of the discipline. Over the last few decades there has been a virtual avalanche of publications of this type. Chapters 3 and 5 have already considered some aspects of such writing, but it is worth looking more closely at several of the problems that characterize it. One of the more obvious is that many of the books that generalize on archaeological topics disappear almost as quickly as they appear. The number of copies printed is usually small, and new editions or even reprints are relatively uncommon. This can sometimes be the case even with books that are hailed by reviewers as models of scholarship. Perhaps this should be expected with many books, given the specialized character of their subjects. Nevertheless, there are others that deserve a better 'life' than they achieve, and it is worth considering what goes wrong. One basic problem, perhaps, is that many contemporary professional archaeologists lack the literary background that some of their predecessors had. Detailed training in faunal analysis or geographical information systems, or in any other of the many specialized aspects of modern archaeology, is not the best way to learn how to write a book. Neither, incidentally, is the writing of a PhD thesis, as many people seem to think. Even the author who has produced numerous impressive papers for journals is not necessarily going to produce an equally impressive general book. The result is that too many of the archaeological syntheses that are published seem to be written by authors who do not actually know how to write. This might seem an outrageous accusation, but the turgid, disorganized, unreadable works that are sometimes produced suggest little familiarity with the great traditions of English literature.

In my opinion, therefore, one of the first requirements for successful synthesis writing is that the author be well read, both within and beyond the archaeological discipline. Such a background can strengthen language use. It can also foster an awareness of the importance of a connective theme, around which the book can be constructed and which can carry the reader on from chapter to chapter. The identification of a central theme of this kind can also help resolve one of the most persistent difficulties of synthesis writing: what we might call the problem of seeing the wood for the trees. The harsh fact is that, whatever topic the author decides to tackle as the subject of a synthesis, the number of relevant published sources is likely to be huge. Sometimes, they can be so numerous that one person could scarcely manage to read them in a lifetime, even if it was possible to access them when needed. Some time ago, for example, an Egyptologist claimed that just to read one year's publications in his discipline would require the reading of four items a day (books or papers but excluding book reviews) for 365 days of the year (Kitchen 1998: 625). In addition, much of the relevant material needed for a synthesis might be written in French or German or Italian, or another language, demanding language skills not possessed by the majority of synthesis writers. Therefore, the secret to writing a good synthesis, if secret there be, is the selection of information that is really significant. The writer who attempts to include everything will either die of old age before finishing the book or, if it is finished, produce an unreadable work mainly useful as a doorstop. A successful synthesis, however, will not only be selective of the data relevant to its theme but will also attempt to present a coherent 'message'. Unfortunately, such an aim has become anathema to some archaeologists, who prefer to edit the disparate products of the discipline's massed word processors to actually advancing an explanation of their own. Similarly, some publishers have taken refuge in huge 'companions' or 'encyclopaedias' of archaeology that include everything but in the long term contribute little. In the end, the main objective of the synthesis writer must be to make sense of a mass of highly complex and varied data. The writer has an obligation to explain the chosen subject to the reader, for it is the writer who has a better chance of doing this than the reader.

So, here we return to the subject of Chapter 3: some writers of archaeological syntheses do not appear to be sure whom they are writing for. Significantly, this is one of the first questions that many publishers ask of a prospective author; they wish to know who the intended readership is to be, because they want to be able to sell copies of the book. The writer might claim that the book is intended for 'the general reader', but it is doubtful if users of public libraries ever see many of the more 'serious' archaeological syntheses and members of the 'public' are disinclined to purchase them. By default, books of this type are mainly read by other archaeologists and by archaeological students. Indeed, in university departments in which academics are unhappy about the mechanical character of many archaeological textbooks, it is general syntheses (as well as journal papers) that students will be encouraged to read instead. Nevertheless, in every generation there will be a handful of archaeologists whose synthetic writing will attract a far wider readership; long ago Penguin Books realized this when they published cheap copies of the works of Gordon Childe and some of his contemporaries. It should be noted, however, that those writers had something to say that attracted readers.

Archaeology in the fast-food age: Writing for the general public

The results of archaeological research are too important to be restricted to academic writing, however generalized. In a grossly overpopulated world where our species has reached plague proportions, so that problems of pollution and environmental degradation are virtually insoluble, there needs to be a greater understanding of how we got that way. Archaeologists are amongst those who have the capacity to explain this and a duty to do so. Unfortunately, however, there is a professional prejudice against what is disparagingly called 'popularization'. In universities, for instance, publications of this sort are unlikely to help in obtaining appointments, tenure, promotions or research grants. It takes courage, therefore, to write for the wider market and considerable skill to identify a target readership correctly. It is significant that some of the more successful authors of 'popular' archaeology have been freelance writers with a journalistic background rather than an academic one. This suggests that writers of this sort of material need a better understanding of possible readership than many professional archaeologists might have. Certainly, if one is to write effectively at this level, it is vital to interest the reader with a text that is readable and understandable by a wide variety of people. This means an avoidance of technical language, an absence of complex grammatical constructions, the use of a familiar vocabulary, the development of an attractive prose style and structure and an imaginative use of illustrations. Care is needed, however, to avoid underestimating readers who might otherwise be alienated by patronizing simplification or by the sort of trivialization that is prevalent in the popular media. Nevertheless, an attempt should also be made to write for that wider media; television, for example, not only contributes to public awareness of archaeological findings but might also improve the status of the archaeological profession in the eyes of the public.

To complicate matters, there is no clear boundary between the scholarly synthesis and the 'popular' book but rather a continuum between the two on which it can be difficult to place some publications. Thus Thames and Hudson's famous 'Ancient Peoples and Places' series, which ran to many volumes between the 1960s and the 1980s, seems to have been intended for non-specialists but was often used by professional archaeologists and students also. Nevertheless, at the popular extreme, many bookshops give the impression that public interest in archaeology is limited to the 'Great Civilizations' and 'Treasures of the Past' type of publication. It seems that there is a continual demand for popular books about Egypt, Mesopotamia, Greece and Rome, and at times about ancient China, India or Mexico. In particular, art and architecture sell, so that even some of the popular books on other parts of the world will tend to be about Australian rock art, Ethiopian churches, Benin bronzes or Tibetan monasteries. So-called mysteries of the past have a particular appeal, Easter Island, for example, being a favourite, although popular books on human evolution also attract public interest. With modern printing technology, most of these books are glossy publications, heavily illustrated in colour but with texts usually not too demanding on the reader. The archaeologist who writes such material will probably find that the publisher will want to decide some of the details. Archaeologists who wish to write a popular book about a subject that is outside the usual perceptions of the human past can find themselves with a tough task. For example, writers on later African societies have grown accustomed to a lack of general interest. No doubt this will continue until archaeologists are able to change the popular image of their discipline. This will take some doing.

As archaeological writers, perhaps we are facing what might be called the 'Hollywood Syndrome'; as the movie industry discovered long ago, the majority of people are interested in fantasy not reality. The actual achievements of millions of men and women who died long ago appear as nothing compared with fairy-story fiction about the historical or prehistoric past. The briefest of inspections of most airport bookstores demonstrates that. Nevertheless, we should not despair entirely. Brian Fagan, for instance, has proved that it is possible to write successful popular books about the human past that are concerned with what actually happened. *The rape of the Nile: Tomb robbers, tourists and archaeologists in Egypt*; and *The long summer: How climate changed civilization*; and *Fish on Friday: Feasting, fasting, and the discovery of the New World*, are just three examples of his many books for a wider readership (Fagan 1975, 2004, 2006b). Furthermore, Fagan has also told us how to produce publications of this sort, in his *Writing archaeology: Telling stories about the past* (Fagan 2006a). Any archaeologist interested in writing what Fagan calls 'trade books' should read that book with care.

Archaeologists also have to accept that, while their profession has been growing more and more concerned with abstruse theories and sophisticated methodologies, many nonarchaeologists have remained fascinated by *things*, by all sorts of items made and used by people in the past. This fascination is apparent from the popularity of television shows about antiques or (horrid word) collectables and even from the archaeologically destructive mania of metal detectorists, who are not necessarily driven by financial gain alone. The excitement of finding things, almost any things, appears to be a deeply engrained human characteristic. Similarly many people are genuinely interested, whether knowledgeable on the subject or not, in ancient structures and sites, so much so that heritage managers often become concerned about tourist blight, the sheer wear and tear on places that the public is determined to love to death. The lesson from all this is that, if archaeological writers want to be read by a wide audience, then they need to write what people want to read. The British publisher of Shire Books has clearly realized this and has produced book after book about the material evidence of the past. Peter Duckers' *British campaign medals 1815–1914* (Duckers 2000) and Robert Copeland's *Blue and white transfer-printed pottery* (Copeland 1998) are two with which I am familiar, but the titles range widely over postmedieval, medieval, Roman and prehistoric subjects, with an emphasis on Britain. The books are very short, well illustrated, have authoritative texts and are inexpensive.

Thus it appears that, rather than archaeologists deciding what the public should read, the public will increasingly decide what they want archaeologists to write for them to read. Indeed, the demand for popular publications will sometimes come from unexpected quarters. For instance, Timothy Owen and Jody Steele, in South Australia, wrote a lively little book for primary-school children and teachers, entitled *Digging up the past: Archaeology for kids*. This book was 'written by two archaeologists who realised how much fun it was playing in the dirt, and how exciting archaeology can be'. They wrote it because of 'the absence of an introductory text about archaeology written for children' (Owen and Steele 2001: 1). Archaeologists who think that such writing is beneath their notice had better not try to write at a popular level.

Conclusion

As suggested by the title of this chapter, the great variety of archaeological publications can make very different demands on any archaeological author who attempts to contribute to all or even a selection of them. Pleasing everyone will require close attention to the diverse character of the readerships involved. Instead, many archaeological authors will understandably concentrate on a more limited range of writing. Nevertheless, whether the approach is broad and generalized or narrow and specialized, it is vital to match one's writing to the task in hand and to the relevant readers. The extent to which this can be achieved will be a major factor in determining the success or otherwise of what you have written.

Eight

Publishers, editors and referees

Devils incarnate or guardian angels?

When an archaeological author has completed a paper or a chapter or a book or some other piece of writing, she or he is apt to feel pleased or at least relieved. 'At least that is over', one is inclined to say to oneself. Nothing could be further from the truth! The real battle has only just begun. Even assuming that the tortures of repeated revisions are over (and that is very doubtful at this stage), there is still the matter of publication. I suspect that all of us start our writing careers somewhat naïve on this subject, and the process of learning can be stressful and there is no escaping its realities. Whether we like it or not, we can find ourselves having to satisfy the requirements of a publisher who is concerned about production costs and marketability, or an editor who wants to 'correct' our English or a referee who dislikes our ideas. I have known archaeologists who have been so incensed by such reactions to their writing that they have responded by throwing it in a drawer and sulking, in some cases for years rather than months. Instead, one needs either to seek another publication outlet or to grit one's teeth and negotiate the problems as far as possible; compromise can be a great healer. In particular, one must attempt to see the situation from the publisher's, editor's or referee's point of view (Derricourt 1996a, 1996b); one must seriously consider that they might actually be right! Might it be that they are not really trying to consign your work to the inferno but to raise it to celestial heights?

Publishing monographs

Let us start with the most prestigious form of publication, the monograph, whether concerned with research or with synthesis. This is somewhat illogical because most archaeological authors will have written a number of papers and lesser contributions before they attempt a full-scale book. Nevertheless, it is books that constitute the largest, most complex and time-consuming form of publication and therefore one deserving priority in this discussion.

The first difficulty is getting started; one has to find a publisher who is willing to risk a considerable amount of money in order to present your work to the reading world. A commissioning editor of a large international publisher, which regularly handles archaeological works, has assured me that a large proportion of what the editors consider for publication is submitted as unsolicited typescripts. Indeed, he told me that this can make their decision easier, particularly with more marginal projects or less experienced authors. There is, therefore, a case for merely sending one's finished work to a publisher without prior discussion. The selection of the publisher can be guided by the character and subject matter of books published by it previously, particularly recent books. However, there is some danger of delay in this strategy. I suppose that there are those authors who might imprudently submit their typescript to more than one publisher at the same time, but I have never done this and I suspect that it could earn one an undesirable reputation. So, one submits one's work and waits for an outcome that, if unfavourable, will mean that one has to start all over again by submitting it to another publisher. My first book (Connah 1975) was a case in point; I submitted it to a well-known American university press that purported to be interested in so-called African Studies, which because the intended book was about the archaeology of Benin

City in Nigeria seemed a good choice. It materialized that it was not. After a year during which I several times appealed for a decision, the publishers rejected it on the grounds that it was too expensive to produce. They were probably right and I did revise it heavily before Clarendon (Oxford University Press) eventually published it, but they could have made up their minds more quickly. Delays of that sort are very discouraging and are particularly unhelpful for an archaeologist early in a career.

With my Benin City book it seems never to have happened, but the process of publishers making up their minds will usually be guided by opinions that they seek from 'readers', other members of the archaeological profession considered to have expertise in the subject area of the intended book. There might be one or more such readers; three seems common and I remember a case where five were involved (but only because two of those first asked were so dilatory in replying). Most readers are people who have published books of their own in the relevant field, and they tend to be chosen because the publisher knows their work. In fact, many of us have been readers as well as authors. Readers' reports will vary in length from a brief paragraph to several detailed pages, and it is common practice for a publisher to transmit them to the author in an anonymous form. If they are uniformly favourable or mostly so, the commissioning editor might then propose the publication of the book to her or his editorial committee, board of directors or other relevant body. Providing it is convinced of the book's viability, the publishing company might then accept the work for publication and send the author a contract. This will set out the length of the book in number of words, the acceptable number and form of illustrations, the expected date of final submission (almost every typescript will need some revision), royalty payments if applicable and sundry other matters. The publisher will expect the author to sign and return this document, which has a legal status.

Inevitably, things are rarely that straightforward. Although readers' reports are often positive rather than negative, they will almost always identify problems in the submitted typescript or suggest additions or deletions. In that case the commissioning editor will ask the author to consider making the appropriate changes to the typescript and the acceptance process will be delayed until these are attended to. In many cases, an author will find it impossible or undesirable to comply with all that has been suggested, but commissioning editors are usually fairly flexible regarding the extent to which they will expect changes to be made on the basis of readers' opinions. There will be some cases, of course, where the readers' reports are so critical that the commissioning editor will conclude that it is undesirable or impractical to proceed further. The editor will then advise the author accordingly, in effect rejecting the submitted typescript. In such a case, the author might merely submit the work to another publisher, but it is wiser to consider the readers' and editor's opinions carefully and do what appears to be necessary to achieve acceptance for publication by the publisher who rejected it or by another publisher. In either event, it is likely that readers' opinions will again be sought and the process repeated.

Writing a proposal for a publisher

Clearly, all this will take time. Depending on circumstances, which can vary enormously, most publishers will make a decision about publication within three to four months, but obviously this time period will be longer if acceptance is conditional on revisions by the author. In that case, timing will depend on how quickly the author can do what is required. The consequent delays can, therefore, be a real problem, and after my experience with my Benin City book, I have always used a different approach. Indeed, whenever I hear of a colleague who has written a book but is 'looking for a publisher' my heart sinks. In my opinion, it is better from an author's point of view to approach a publisher before writing a particular book and to discuss your idea with its representative, usually a commissioning editor who in larger publishing companies will be a specialist in archaeological, historical, anthropological or general humanities subjects. If the editor likes the idea, she or he will very likely suggest that you submit a written proposal concerning the book. In practice, I have found it preferable to write a proposal before contacting a publisher, so that the relevant editor can be given a detailed description of the proposed work at the time that you first make contact. This will also give the editor an opportunity to make suggestions about the planned book, suggestions that can often be of assistance to the author, who might then revise the proposal accordingly. I cannot emphasize strongly enough how important it is to write that proposal with great care. Its content, argument, organization and English expression have to convince the editor, and the readers to whom it will be sent, that you are proposing to write something that is worthwhile and that you have the ability to do it. No doubt, others will have different ideas about how to write such a proposal, but I have developed a particular formula that seems to be successful.

I commence with a brief introduction of one paragraph that says what the book is to be about and how it will contribute to archaeological scholarship or to the interests of general readers. This is followed by the main body of the proposal that consists of a chapter-by-chapter description of the intended book, usually devoting one substantial paragraph to each chapter and heading each paragraph with the number and title of the chapter. These chapter descriptions need considerable thought and careful writing; they are in effect abstracts of chapters that do not yet exist. As discussed in Chapter 7, a good abstract is one that provides a précis of a piece of writing, not merely telling the reader what it is about but stating what it contributes. Many authors find abstract writing difficult, but it can be particularly difficult when it is a précis of something that has not yet been written. Thus, to be able to write a description of each chapter, it is obvious that the intending author must have given considerable thought to the structure and content of the proposed book.

The next section of the proposal should indicate the intended length of the book, in thousands of words, bearing in mind that 90,000–100,000 words are usually considered to be a full-length book and 50,000–60,000 words a short book. It should be made clear whether the stated number of words is for the text only or for the text and the reference list and captions, as some publishers will require. There should also be some indication of the likely number of tables, if appropriate, and their complexity. In addition, the sort of in-text referencing to be employed should be indicated, as well as the character and likely size of the reference list. If footnotes or endnotes and a glossary are to be included, these should be mentioned, as well as any special text layout features such as the increasingly popular 'boxes'. If an index is likely to be necessary, it should be stated whether the author is willing to prepare it, because publishers are usually unwilling to do so. With almost all archaeological books, illustrations are important, so this section should also state the proposed number of figures, specifying how many are expected to be line drawings and how many are expected to be photographs. The numbers will obviously vary with the subject, but in my own experience about 100 figures might be appropriate for a full-length book and about 50 figures for a short book, with about half of the total consisting of photographs in each case. Concerning the illustrations it will also be wise to indicate if any of them will need printing in colour (no longer the near-impossible expectation that it used to be) and whether any will require special treatment such as 'fold-outs' (an expensive luxury that is rarely possible). Clearly, all these details can vary enormously with the character and purpose of the book; in order to provide appropriate specifications the intending author would be wise to examine a selection of comparable archaeological books, to see what other authors have done.

The proposal should then have a section that every commissioning editor will be anxious to see. You should try to identify the intended readership of the book: is it to be students and professional archaeologists only, or is it to be more 'general' readers? Where are these people; if students for instance, how many relevant university departments are there and in which countries? It might even be possible to list some of the departments that are most likely to be interested. Furthermore, is the book likely to be bought by individual readers or only by libraries? In addition, it is a good idea to give the titles of already published books on the same or a related subject and comment on how they differ from the one that you propose to write. This is particularly worth doing if comparable books were published some time ago or are out of print. Inevitably, there will be a temptation to exaggerate in this section but this should be avoided; the editor who reads your proposal will have read many others previously and is unlikely to be deceived by overstatement.

Finally, the proposal should end with a brief section that provides an outline timetable for writing the book and indicates a likely submission date for the finished typescript and illustrations. You might even specify the intended form of the submitted typescript: word-processed, double-spaced, correction-free text on paginated A4 sheets with wide margins being usual, together with a digital version on disc in some widely used software. Similarly the form in which the illustrations will be supplied might be indicated: whether hard copy only or both hard copy and digital format, and in the latter case stating the software to be employed. At its end the proposal should also contain details of your postal address, your e-mail address, your telephone number, your fax number if you have one and your mobile number, as well as an indication of your probable movements over the months to come. It is remarkable how often such details can be overlooked and how aggravating this can be for an editor who reads a proposal.

In my opinion, it is unwise for the entire proposal to exceed twenty single-sided pages of A4 paper with a text of 1.5-line spacing: single-spacing can discourage a reader and double-spacing is unnecessary. It is also important that the layout of the proposal be logical, clear, neat and without errors or corrections: one is trying to encourage someone to actually read it and at the same time trying to convince that person that you know what you are talking about. Indeed, one might go further in this respect and provide two or three sample chapters of the proposed book, but this will entail a great deal more work that at this early stage might not be practicable. If you have had contact with an editor prior to writing the proposal, sample chapters might even be requested, particularly from beginning authors (and even from some more experienced) because the editor wishes to find out if you can actually write. When submitting the proposal, at least one hard copy should be sent, as well as a digital version on disc. If the publisher's editor thinks that your proposition is viable, the proposal (and sample chapters if provided) will then be sent out to readers and, as already discussed, a generally favourable response will eventually result in the offer of a contract. However, from the publisher's point of view there is inevitably a risk associated with issuing a contract merely on the basis of a proposal and perhaps several sample chapters. The completed book, when it is submitted, might be different from what was proposed. Indeed, the very act of writing a book will often cause an author to modify its intended structure, content or interpretations. Nevertheless, I have never heard of a case where a publisher rejected a submitted work on these grounds, although I suppose that somewhere in the fine print of the average contract there is provision for such an outcome.

Interaction between authors and publishers

The relationship between an author and a publisher's editor is an important one, which can influence the character and even the quality of the book that is eventually published. The preface or the acknowledgements section in many archaeological books records the author's appreciation of an editor's input. In contrast, many years ago I knew a senior academic archaeologist who swore that all publishers had horns and tails and were responsible for everything that went wrong in his books. I suspected at the time that most of his perceived problems were of his own making, but (tactfully) did not express my opinion in his presence. It seems that academics, in particular, can sometimes combine disorganization and arrogance in a manner that a hard-pressed editor can find difficult to deal with. In the late 1960s, for instance, there was a noted archaeologist who submitted an important book to one of the major international academic publishers that was in such a chaotic mess that, it was rumoured, the publisher declined to publish archaeological works for several years thereafter. I also recollect an instance when my own writing was running behind as a contract submission date approached. When I wrote apologetically to the editor, saying that the book would be several months late, I received a reply that said that I should not worry too much; a book from another author had recently arrived eleven years late and without its reference list!

My own experience of dealing with editors has generally been a happy one; I have much enjoyed working with some, although I have occasionally had to deal with others who seemed to regard an author as a nuisance who was best ignored as much as possible. This latter tendency has, I suspect, been one of the consequences of publishing being increasingly handled by large multinational companies, whose major concern appears to be profit. As an author, I have often found it useful to sit down with an editor and talk face-to-face about the book that I am working on, in which, after all, we both have a common interest. As publishers have grown larger, however, that sort of personal contact seems to have become less welcomed by them. With some smaller, more specialized companies it can, no doubt, still be found, although an author must bear in mind that the smaller the company, the more limited the marketing and distribution of the book are likely to be. I suspect that in the past things were generally more personal than they have now become. In the late 1970s, for instance, Grahame Clark told me how he came to write his book *Prehistoric England* (Clark 1944–1945) that was first published in 1940. From what I remember, he said that one Sunday morning in the late 1930s he and his wife were sitting in the cottage in which they lived somewhere outside Cambridge, when they were unexpectedly visited by B. T. Batsford, the publisher of a famous series of books on English heritage. Batsford asked Clark to write a book for the general public about prehistoric England and offered him something like £100 to do it. So poor were academic salaries at that time that the offer was immediately accepted and the result was a book that was part of a turning point in archaeological interpretation. In such a way is history sometimes made.

Publishing papers

So far, I have discussed professional editors employed by commercial publishers. The archaeological author will, however, frequently deal with editors who, to varying degrees, are not full-time specialists. For instance, academics, or museum workers or other professional archaeologists, who undertake editing in their 'spare time', edit many archaeological journals. Such editors are often highly experienced and in no way should they be regarded as 'amateurs' at the task, but in the very best sense that is what they are. The result is that the archaeological author should expect very variable treatment from those who 'run' many of the archaeological journals. There might be delays in acknowledging the receipt of a paper or in sending it out to referees, and the general level of communication can sometimes be poor, although e-mail has improved this. Authors have often had some editorial experience themselves, and they need to remember that a journal editor probably has to fit the editorial work into the time-consuming business of earning a living by other means.

For many, this will mean that editing is limited to evenings and weekends. Some larger international journals are able to employ professional editorial assistants, who can carry some of the load, but for many smaller or more specialized journals this is not the case.

As discussed in Chapters 3 and 7, it is important for an author to choose the most suitable journal for a paper depending on its subject, but it is also useful to be aware of a journal editor's particular interests. This means that it is helpful for the author to know the editor and something of the editor's background and personality. One editor might publish a paper even if it conflicts with her or his own views, whereas another might not welcome such a paper and might reject it or at least try to persuade the author to change it. Some editors are very tolerant of varying prose styles; others might try to correct the author's English or attempt to modify it to suit a particular readership in America, or Britain or in some other part of the English-speaking world. In extreme cases, editors can come to regard 'their' journal as almost personal property, and there have even been instances where it appears that a new journal has been started mainly as a means of promoting its editor and her or his personal interests and opinions. As a result, authors can find some journal editors much easier to work with than others and might even publish a succession of papers in the same journal at least partly for this reason. Indeed, it can sometimes happen that so good a relationship is built up with a journal editor that an author will be requested to write a paper on a specific subject, although such a request can also come from an editor unknown to the author. In my own case, I can remember journal editors whose ability, efficiency and courtesy were exemplary. Unfortunately there have been others whom I would prefer not to remember at all!

Some journal editors are remarkably effective; I know of one who edits more than 1,000 pages of published material a year, although with some editorial assistance. To that can be added twice as much again, material that is not accepted for publication or is delayed while revision takes place, but still has to be read with care. This is a truly amazing achievement, particularly when one considers that there have been some journal editors who have 'carried' a journal for ten or more years without a break. There is, however, another type of nonprofessional editing that lacks such continuity. This is the editing of what was referred to in Chapter 3 as the 'collected' volume. The editors of such collections of papers vary greatly, from highly experienced professional archaeologists, who have authored many of their own papers and might also have previously been a journal editor, to complete novices who have had little publication experience and none at all of editing. There is a particular tendency for some younger academics to think that editing a collected volume is the way to fame and fortune. They seem to regard editing as easy; all you have to do is write to a few friends asking for papers and then put them all together. Unless they learn quickly that this is not the case, the outcome can be unfortunate. So, authors should beware; it is wise to find out something about the proposed editor (or editors, this sort of publication is frequently handled by several people) before agreeing to submit a paper. It is also a good idea to enquire into the publication prospects of such a volume; instances are known where projects have faded out or died abruptly. In such cases the editor or editors are not always to blame, but inexperience can often be a contributory factor.

Common to most sorts of editing, except that of some newsletters, conference proceedings and collected volumes, is the use of readers or referees to assess the scholarly quality of a book or paper, in order to decide whether it is acceptable for publication. Readers for publishers have been discussed earlier, but it is referees acting for journal editors whom the archaeological author will most frequently have to deal with. If a journal editor actually 'commissions' an author to write a paper on a particular subject, then it might be published without refereeing, but mere professional seniority and experience do not exempt an author from this process. In effect, the editor is seeking an independent opinion about the author's work. Journal referees are usually sought amongst the author's peers, and editors will often seek more than one person to act in this role. In theory, such 'peer review' plays a vital part in quality control for the advancement of knowledge and scholarship. In practice, the situation is somewhat more complex.

There is the danger, for instance, that referees with conservative views might discourage publication of innovative work that is subsequently found to be of importance. There is even the risk of a malicious response because the writing in question impinges on or contradicts published or unpublished work by the referee. More commonly, those giving opinions in this way might question aspects of the writing under review merely because they would have written it differently; in other words they will be insufficiently objective. In recent decades, there has been a tendency for this to happen particularly because of theoretical disagreements. Another disadvantage of the system is that at any one time an enormous number of referees' reports are being sought, so that an unreasonable number of requests are made of some individuals (who are not paid for this service) and responses are substantially delayed or in some cases never received at all. Finally, the outcome of a refereeing process will inevitably be influenced by the journal editor's choice of referees. Not only will some of them be better informed on a specific subject than others, but some will be generally more tolerant and others more critical. Thus a lot might depend on the editor's knowledge of the archaeological profession, as well as the editor acting in good faith and choosing referees most likely to give a fair judgement of the author's work. It has been claimed that 'The peer-review system for publication in science journals is inherently flawed and in desperate need of an overhaul' (Hendrickx 2008: 10), but the overall refereeing process does work fairly well in the circumstances. Sooner or later all of us come up against a referee who is a misanthropic pedant or one whose comments are so ambiguous that they are useless, but fortunately referees are also authors themselves and are therefore apt to recollect the biblical injunction (Luke 6: 31) to do unto others as you would be done by.

Reports by referees are sent to the journal editor who has requested them. She or he will then send the reports to the author, indicating whether the paper is acceptable for publication in its submitted form, or is only acceptable following revision along the lines suggested in the reports or is considered unsuitable for publication for reasons indicated in the reports. When sending the reports to the author, the editor will try to ensure that the anonymity of the referees is maintained and in some cases might even delete parts of a report that are judged to be malicious, slanderous, insulting or gratuitously unkind. Some years ago I edited a journal where I also tried to ensure the anonymity of the author, by removing her or his name from the typescript sent to the referees, but this proved impractical because referees could usually identify the writer from the subject of the paper. If an author is asked to revise work in accordance with referees' reports, an editor will also usually append some guiding comments, indicating the extent to which she or he agrees with the reports and to what extent the author should revise. However, it can be difficult for editors if they disagree with the reports that they receive. I can recollect occasions when an editor has decided to ignore negative reports and publish a paper that has been recommended for rejection. This can anger the referees whose opinions have been ignored and in one instance is claimed to have contributed to the replacement of an editor, when it subsequently materialized that the referees had given the right advice and that it was the editor who had got it wrong.

The final stage of this editorial and refereeing saga is, of course, the author's response to the opinions, sometimes clumsily expressed, of others. Some authors might throw a tantrum, and others change as little as possible, but the wise author will weigh and consider with great care the things that have been said. In my own case I have usually found that referees' comments were of three sorts: those with which I agreed and to which I was willing to attend, those with which I agreed but which I could not deal with unless I wrote a different paper and those with which I disagreed because they were wrong or because they conflicted fundamentally with my own opinions. Most journal editors are quite tolerant regarding the extent to which an author makes changes in accordance with referees' comments, providing it is apparent that a genuine effort has been made to attend to the more important of them. For the author this can require revision, more revision and yet more revision.

Conclusion

Revision is vital for good writing; it is essential to listen to criticism and to respond appropriately. This is a subject that has been touched on previously in this book and will need more detailed discussion in the next chapter, to which we must now turn. The publishers, editors and readers or referees, who have been the subject of this chapter, will usually ensure that adequate revision is undertaken, in our interest as well as theirs. In the end, they are indeed on the side of the angels.

Nine

The publication process

Creating a quality product

The archaeological author will soon discover that it is important to learn as much as possible about the publication process. After the labour of writing and revising and finding an interested book publisher or journal editor, it will be a tragedy if the published result is poorly produced. In many cases when this does happen it is because the author's understanding of the process has been inadequate, although there are publishers and editors who could ruin almost anything without assistance from an author. If this is to be avoided and if a quality product is to result, then each must understand what the other wants, and to do this they must be able to communicate, often at short notice. The problem is that the publication process can vary from case to case and has changed as printing technology has evolved, as the use of computers has become widespread and as the commercial organization of publishing has altered. Efficient publishers and journals will usually inform the author, soon after the final acceptance of a typescript, of the various stages of production or refer the author to their Web site for details. As with the writing process discussed in Chapter 5, many details of the publication process can also be found in relevant manuals. Of these, *Handbook for academic authors* by Beth Luey (Luey 2002) is an example, and an old favourite of mine is the *Style manual: For authors, editors and printers* (2002). The latter has gone through numerous editions and is respected in other parts of the world as well as in its Australian homeland. An alternative is *The Oxford style manual* (Ritter 2003). In addition, Robin Derricourt's guide to scholarly publishing deserves special attention because of the author's archaeological background (Derricourt 1996a, 1996b). This chapter can hardly compete with sources such as these, but it will provide an outline of the essential aspects of the author–publisher relationship based on my own experience.

The submitted typescript

Your submitted typescript must be clean, double-spaced copy, prepared in the manner specified by the publisher or journal. A4-size paper should be used unless something different is required. The pages must be single-sided paginated and it is now common practice to submit both hard copy and digital copy. The latter will usually be on a CD or DVD, but in some cases can be submitted as an attachment to an e-mail message. With all digital copy it is essential to ascertain the types of software that are acceptable to the publisher or journal and to indicate clearly what you have used. The submitted material must be absolutely complete: in the case of a book, for instance, usually consisting of half-title page, title page, dedication, contents list, figures list, tables list, acknowledgements, preface and/or foreword, main text, reference list, and list of figure captions. The order of the 'Preliminaries', or 'Prelims' as they are often called, should follow usual conventions or the specific instructions of the publisher. Usually this material is not included in the pagination of the text. The tables should be separate from the rest of the typescript, and figures should also be separate and numbered in sequence. Tables and illustrations can also be submitted as digital copy, although many publishers and editors still ask for hard copies also. However, illustrations should not be sent as PDFs because of the loss of quality that will result. Whatever form the illustrations are in, it is important to submit the highest quality attainable. It is also wise to make it clear from the beginning if you need illustrations returned following publication, perhaps for reuse in future writing. Some publishers and editors will actually send an author a checklist of what they need submitted and how they want it done. Overall, the more care that you take with the submission of your material, the more likely it is that the publication process will be trouble-free. Editors love authors who are well organized; it means less work for them.

Obtaining copyright permissions

A matter of importance is the copyright of illustrations that you have used or of text that you have quoted at length. Most publishers and journal editors will expect you to have already obtained permission to use such material and might require you to produce written evidence of this when you submit your work for publication. Copyright laws vary from country to country, and it is safest to seek permission for any illustrations of which you are not yourself the originator. Illustration copyright permissions were discussed in Chapter 6, but according to the Berne Convention you will also need to seek permission for any textual quotations of 800 words or longer, as either an aggregate or a single item, from a single published source. Editors prefer authors to seek any necessary permissions rather than themselves, because copyright holders are more likely to charge them a fee than to charge an author. Thus care is needed when selecting material that will need copyright clearance. Authors will also have to be remarkably patient; as discussed in Chapter 6, obtaining permission can be a time-consuming and frustrating business. In addition, copyright permissions are normally given for world rights in the English language only and for only one edition of a book; if an author wants to publish a translation of a work or bring out a new edition, the process will have to be started all over again. Such are the problems that there is nearly always a residue of unanswered requests, making it necessary to include in the acknowledgements a statement saying that every effort was made to obtain all copyright permissions and in cases where this could not be done the publisher and author request that they be contacted.

The stages of production

As already stated, soon after the final acceptance of a typescript and providing it has no problems, efficient publishers and journals will usually inform the author about the various stages of production. Because of the greater complexity of the process, this is more commonly done by book publishers. They will often send the author a schedule listing the dates by which: copy editing will be completed, design and layout finished, the work delivered to the printer, proofs sent to the author, index copy made available by the author, index proofs sent to the author, printed copies sent for binding, copies of the book made available in stock and publication achieved by the release of copies for sale. The timetable might be less detailed than this, but the publisher will expect the author to keep to those parts of it that require an author's response. This is particularly the case now, because the publisher, copy editor, design and layout specialist, printer, binder and marketing department might each be different companies in different cities, or sometimes even in different countries, and any delays can prove costly.

As the first stage in this lengthy process, the book will be handed to a copy editor, who will ensure that it conforms to the house style of the publisher and will ask the author to attend to any problems of expression or other perceived weaknesses. Copy editors are often contracted by the publisher, frequently have a background in the relevant or a related discipline, and have a difficult job to do. I once knew a particularly belligerent agricultural scientist who, when sent a list of copy editor's queries by a leading international publisher, is reputed to have replied with a telegram that read, 'Tell the copy editor bloke to fix it himself and have a few beers out of the royalties.' This is not recommended as a strategy! Instead, an author should respond immediately and be as helpful as possible. After all, the copy editor is a specialist who is almost certainly more expert than the author at picking out problems that might annoy readers or delight the sort of book reviewer who likes to find mistakes. To understand the importance of the copy editor's work, an author should consult Judith Butcher's *Copy-editing: The Cambridge handbook* (Butcher 1981). Some journal papers are also subject to specialist copy editing, but the editors of smaller journals often undertake the task themselves, along with everything else.

Once an author has answered all the copy editor's questions and agreed about consequent changes to the book or paper (and authors should beware of copy editors who make alterations without consultation), the submitted material will be passed to a production team, sometimes part of a different commercial operation from the publisher. This team will deal with typography, typesetting, paper selection, layout and overall design. For archaeological publications a most important part of this work is the sizing and location of illustrations and tables. In particular, there is a real danger that figures will be overreduced or unsuitably positioned. If the production team members are particularly good at their job, and if as author you are very lucky, they might even consult you regarding the reduction and reproduction of the illustrations, but many archaeologists find that they do not get enough feedback on these matters. Probably this is because those doing the work are wary of authors who might cause expensive delays or make impossible demands. So, if you are consulted on such matters make sure that you respond immediately and realistically, taking all the circumstances into consideration. Eventually, when the production people have done what they have to do, your work will be passed to a printer, again often a different business.

So, the next time that you hear about your book or paper will be when the proofs arrive. Those of us who have been publishing for many years can remember the days when one had both 'galley proofs' and 'page proofs', the latter appearing after the corrections from the galleys had been made. Galley proofs were about a half-metre long and consisted of a single column of continuous text, which had not yet been divided into pages. This was when loose print was handset in a printer's tray known as a galley, or set in bars of type from a linotype machine. As a result, proof-reading could be a grim experience: I once counted more than a hundred errors in a galley from a particularly incompetent printer and can even recall seeing a whole line of type set upside down. In addition, one frequently had to put a ring around individual letters and an 'X' in the margin to indicate type that was damaged and required changing. Fortunately, these problems are now in the past; page proofs are now the only sort, and digital typesetting has made errors rare. In some cases the proofs will not even be on paper, but will be sent out electronically as a PDF. Nevertheless, the author still needs to 'read' the proofs; I once saw a paper, in a journal that had been digitally set, in which a whole paragraph had been printed twice, suggesting that nobody had checked the proofs. It was, I am glad to say, not a paper of mine!

Correcting proofs

The question is, How should an author check her or his proofs? Opinions vary widely on this subject, although some authors seem reluctant to admit what they do. An historian whom I knew said that all he did was to read the proofs through and correct anything that looked wrong or check it against the original. In contrast, I formerly had a secretary who had previously worked for a professor of English literature, with whom she cross-read the proofs of an entire book out loud, backwards! This strategy was to counteract a psychological problem that causes one to miss errors because one reads what should be there, rather than what is actually there: a failure that is particularly likely to occur because of the boredom of the task and the time that it takes. I doubted the truth of this story until I met someone else who had come across the same method, but it still seems impractical to me. In my own case, I have customarily checked proofs by cross-reading them (forwards) with another person, usually my unfortunate wife. She will read out loud slowly from the type-script, and I will listen carefully whilst reading the proof. This can be mind numbing and tiring work. Furthermore, it can take a number of days to proof-read a whole book. Nevertheless, it is the most practical way that I know of to produce an error-free or near error-free text. Even the smallest error can be most unfortunate; I recall a publication where a man was said to have 'moderate tastes' but the proof-reader had missed the fact that the 'a' had been printed as an 'e'.

Proof-reading can be particularly difficult if the publisher or editor has failed to supply you with a final copy-edited version of the text, in the form that it was sent to the printer. This can happen if the copy editor has not consulted with you as the author. In my opinion this is unforgivable, because it forces the author to read the proofs against the typescript as it was prior to copy editing. It then becomes very difficult to be sure which are the copy editor's alterations and which are possible errors by the printer. It is the latter that proof-reading by the author is intended to correct, and publishers and editors routinely remind authors that proof-reading should not be used as an occasion to alter the text in any way; this stage is far too late for revision. Indeed, some publishers will go so far as to require authors to make their corrections to the proofs with different coloured pens, such as red for printer's errors, blue for any author's errors previously overlooked and green for any essential last-minute changes to the text. The last type of change should be avoided and the extra printing costs that they cause can be charged to an author, although I have never heard of it happening. In some cases editors or printers might tell an author that they will also be reading the proofs, but it is unwise for an author to use this as an excuse to give the task less attention; there is no way of knowing how thoroughly they will do the job. However, occasionally they can overdo it; there was an obvious error in one of my books because at the last minute a copy editor, reading the proofs, mistakenly changed a word that was thought to be incorrect and neglected to inform me until the material had gone back to the printer and it was too late to correct it. In fact, timing is of the essence in proof-reading. The author will be given a deadline by which the proofs must be returned; it is most unwise to fail to meet this because printers will sometimes merely proceed without the corrections or with only those made by themselves.

A particularly nasty part of proof-reading is dealing with bibliographies/lists of references: errors seem to breed in them like flies. Inconsistent use of italics, of capital letters, of punctuation; incorrect dates of publication; misspelling of authors' names; wrong volume numbers; mistakes in pagination: the possibilities are numerous. Almost always an assiduous proof-reader will find things needing correction amongst the references. Personally, I do not cross-read them out loud with another person, as I do with the main text. It is more efficient to put the proof side by side with the typescript and compare it visually line by line. When checking such proofs or, indeed, any other proofs of text or tables or figure captions, it is important to use the internationally accepted proof-correcting symbols, in the margins of the page and amongst the type itself. These will be found published in many places, of which the *Style manual: For authors, editors and printers* (2002) is a good place to look. If it is necessary to provide an instruction to the typesetter or ask a question, it should be written in the margin and circled to indicate that it is not additional matter to be inserted in the text but is merely a communication from the author.

There are other things to consider when correcting proofs. It is important, for instance, to check the illustrations and their captions. More than one archaeological book or paper has been published with the wrong caption under an illustration. The quality, positioning and orientation of illustrations also need close examination. If illustrations are too dark, or too light or too much reduced, they will not do their intended job, and this needs to be pointed out by the author at the proof stage. The publisher and printer might not be able to improve the quality for technical reasons or might be unwilling to try, but such problems must be brought to their attention. Occasionally there will even be major problems such as an illustration printed upside down; vertical aerial photographs (conventionally printed with north at the top) are particularly likely to be treated in this way. In such cases the author must insist that the matter be rectified. Another task that the author might need to attend to at the proof stage is the provision of 'running headlines', which are often printed in the top margin of each page in a book or journal paper. In books, these might consist of a short title of the book on the verso and a short title of the chapter on the recto; in journals it can be a short title of the paper on the verso and the author's name on the recto. However, content can vary depending on the character of the publication and personal choice. Running headlines are usually done by the editor or copy editor for both books and journal papers, but the author will sometimes be asked to supply them, ideally in separate lists for the verso and recto pages and with the relevant page number for each headline. It is essential that each headline is short enough to fit comfortably within the width of the printed page, and to leave space for the page number if the pagination is at the top of the page.

It is also at the proof stage that the index of a book must be prepared, if an index is necessary as is often the case in archaeological books. This is because it is only now that final page numbers are available. However, the indexer should have previously prepared a detailed list of subjects for the index, in order not to delay the return of the proofs with which the typescript of the index must be sent. If subjects have already been listed, then all that needs to be done at this stage is to add the relevant page numbers to each index entry, but even this can take a lot of time. Most publishers will wish to avoid the expense of indexing and will expect authors to prepare the index themselves or arrange for others to do it. Professional indexers do exist and for one of my books I employed such a person, but it is better if someone more familiar with the subject does the indexing. Family members are often enlisted for the task; in my case I owe my wife Beryl a considerable amount of gratitude for compiling more indexes over the years than either of us can remember. There are publications that explain how to go about the task, of which once again the *Style manual: For authors, editors and printers* (2002) is one of the more useful. Nowadays there is also software that allows the construction of an index on a computer, a method that makes the job easier. Nevertheless, indexing remains difficult, particularly the grouping of subject entries. The task needs great care if a book is not to be spoilt by an inaccurate or unusable index. One of the last tasks for a book author will be to check the proofs of the index, a job that requires close attention.

The dust jacket or cover and other matters

Another task for an author late in the publication process of a book is likely to be checking its dust jacket (on hardbacks) or cover (on paperbacks). As mentioned in Chapter 5, publishers tend to be concerned about book titles because they can affect sales, and for the same reason they give close attention to a book's dust jacket or cover. When submitting a book to a publisher, I have often suggested one of its more interesting illustrations for use on its jacket or cover. Sometimes my suggestion has been adopted, sometimes not. Publishers go to some trouble about this matter, with the dust jacket or cover often being specially designed, sometimes not very appropriately. Fortunately, an author will usually be sent a proof of the jacket or cover, and when this is received it is important to look at it closely. Some years ago, a book about the archaeology of Meroë, in the Sudan, had a map on its jacket that showed the site in the wrong place; the designer had confused it with another place with a similar name (Shinnie 1967). The error had gone unnoticed until too late. On another occasion, an author's name was misspelled on the jacket but luckily that was corrected! A further problem that can occur is the printing of a title on the jacket or cover that differs from that on the title page of the book.

Apart from the front of the jacket or cover, there will also be text on its back that needs proofing. This will usually consist of a short description of the book's contents, a description that the author will probably have written at the request of the publisher earlier in the publication process. Traditionally, this description was intended for the bookshop customer who pulled the book off a shelf to look at it when deciding whether to purchase it or not. Perhaps less important now that so much book selling is on-line, it is still customary for the description to be present, sometimes followed by several short quotations from well-known archaeologists saying what a good book it is! Below there is often a brief laudatory description of the author; unsurprisingly, this is usually written by the author. Either on the back of the jacket or cover or on its inside there might also be a photograph of the author, often taken years ago before the passage of time and too much writing had taken their toll. Finally, the spine of the jacket and the cover will have a usually abbreviated title of the book and the name of the author. All of this dust-jacket or cover material needs to be examined very closely at proof stage; it is most unfortunate if errors in it go undetected.

At some stage in the publication process, often towards its end and sometimes at the time of publication, many book publishers will seek information from the author that will help to market the book. This might even be in the form of a questionnaire to which the author will be requested to respond. The publisher will seek advice about university departments and other institutions to which free copies might be sent. The author might also be asked to list journals and other publications that might publish reviews of the book and that therefore should be sent review copies. In addition, the publisher might want to know whether there are imminent archaeological conferences where the book might be displayed or at least information about its publication be made available. Similarly, the publisher might wish to know whether a book launch is likely to be organized, although publishers rarely undertake to do this themselves. In many cases the publisher will also have a 'flyer' printed, a single sheet of paper giving details of the book, its author and how to purchase it. The author will usually be asked to check a proof of this flyer before it is released. Also at this time, the author might request the publisher to send free copies of the book to a small number of people who were particularly helpful during its writing or who required a copy as a condition of granting copyright clearance for illustrations or quotations.

Print-ready material

Because publication can vary so greatly, some details in this chapter are not relevant. Some publishers, for instance, insist that authors do their own layout of a book, complete with illustrations, tables, list of references and correct formatting, so that it is ready for the printer. This considerably reduces publishing costs, although it is likely to increase the author's costs. For instance, with such a publication neither copy editing nor proofing will be necessary because the author will, in effect, have done all of that prior to submission. This method of publication also speeds up the publication process; I have had traditionally published books take anything from eight to thirty months to appear, although modern printing technology is shortening such time. Ready-to-print books, in contrast, can appear in three to four months. This method of publication is particularly suitable for very specialized material that is likely to have only limited sales; *British Archaeological Reports* are a remarkable example of what can be achieved. However, preparing ready-to-print material takes a lot of the author's time and can present many technical difficulties. I have even laid out a book in French for a Parisian publisher, not an activity that I would recommend (Connah 2008).

Publication in journals

Much of the discussion in this chapter applies to books of one sort or another, rather than to journal papers and other shorter pieces of writing that form the bulk of the material published by most archaeologists. Nevertheless, the publication process is similar in such matters as submission, copy editing, layout, type-setting, printing and proofing. The main differences are those of scale. This varies with the financial circumstances and circulation of the journal or other outlet to which one is contributing. As mentioned in Chapter 8, archaeologists who have other full-time jobs and varied editorial experience edit many of the journals and other composite publications. Publishing companies, with professional editors and support staff, produce others, much in the same way that they produce books. Consequently, the author's involvement in the publication process can vary; editors of small journals might require more input from authors than editors of larger, more commercial ones, who will prefer that they or their staff handle most of the details. Thus, with these sorts of publications it is perhaps even more important that authors understand the particular publication process that operates, simply because it can be different in each case. Failure to understand the relevant process can inconvenience the hard-pressed editor of a smaller journal or alienate the editor of a larger one. In neither case is the outcome likely to be of advantage to the author.

Conclusion

It needs to be emphasized that, after many years of relative stasis, the publication process and especially printing technology are now changing so rapidly that they are difficult to keep up with. For this and the other reasons discussed in this chapter, it is most important that the archaeological author learns as much as possible about the process that will turn a particular typescript and its illustrations into a published work. This will not happen by magic and assuming that it will can result in disaster!

Ten

The aftermath

Reviewers and readers

The book or the paper or the other piece of writing is published, it is out there in the big wide world, but what now? Most authors probably experience elation at the time of publication, but sadly, it is usually short-lived. It is quickly replaced by a feeling of uncertainty about the progeny whose gestation has been so important to them. Will anybody read it? Was anything overlooked that should have been included? Could it have been better written? These and other questions might worry the author, but of course, it is all too late. So, one waits for feedback; one waits to see what other people think of one's work. In my own experience, it is very difficult to judge the quality of your own writing; you cannot be sufficiently objective about something that you have been so close to for so long. On rare occasions you might feel that you did a good job; more commonly you suspect that you could have done a better one. Significantly, years later you might reread something you wrote and be pleasantly surprised at its quality or acutely embarrassed by its shortcomings. At the time of publication, however, you are dependent on the judgement of others.

For books, the first to pass judgement are often book reviewers. In the case of archaeological writing, reviews are mostly published in professional journals concerned with the discipline, but sometimes they appear in the journals of related subjects such as history or anthropology and occasionally in more general media such as magazines and newspapers. A successful fiction writer once claimed that he had never read reviews of his books after a poor review of the first one, which went on to sell a half-million copies. Perhaps he had a point; some reviews can undermine an author's confidence in a quite unjustifiable fashion. Nevertheless, as archaeologists, we must grit our teeth and read every review that appears of our work. Indeed, we should be grateful if a reviews editor of a journal (particularly a major one) thinks that our book is important enough to send out for review because, for reasons of space, not every book received for review is actually reviewed. We should be even more grateful if a reviews editor decides that our book justifies the commissioning of a 'review article', a short paper that uses a discussion of the book as a starting point for an examination of wider issues in the discipline. As remarked in Chapter 3, the authors of archaeological books sometimes complain that people who have never written a book themselves often write reviews. True or false, book reviews have an important role to play as commentaries on our work. Most reviews will first summarize what the book is about and then comment on its treatment of the subject, its presentation of data, its interpretations, its theoretical basis and so on. Following this, a reviewer might discuss the book's structure, the author's writing style, the quality of the illustrations and tables, the standard of the printing and the overall quality of the book's production. However, reviews vary greatly in their character, from those that describe the book without saying what the reviewer thinks about it, to those that either praise or condemn the book or do something in between. There are even reviews that seem to be mainly intended to show how much more the reviewer knows about the subject than the unfortunate author.

The people who read book reviews usually do so in order to keep up with current publications in their areas of interest and to decide whether they should purchase a copy of a particular book, or look for it in a library or just ignore it. Therefore, it is probable that reviews do have an influence on book sales. At least many publishers seem to believe this because they will often collect reviews for their files, and more considerate publishers will even send a copy of each review to the author in case she or he has not seen it. In response, an author should send copies of known reviews to the publishers, in case they have missed them. Publishers are interested in reviews of a book because reviews provide them with information about its professional reception. In particular, favourable reviews supply the publishers with material from which they can quote remarks that praise the book, often printing them on the back of any reprints or new editions. The more eminent the reviewer, the more likely it is that this will be done. Unfavourable reviews are another matter. One that I read recently, about a book concerned with an aspect of European archaeology, contained the following comments: 'This book is a mess. It shows inaccuracy, lack of rigour, stating the obvious and sloppy writing' (Hummler 2007: 1122). It is unknown how the author and publishers reacted.

Journal papers and other smaller publications are usually not reviewed, although some journals like to print 'forums', in which a selection of specialists will respond briefly to a particular paper, after which the original author will be allowed to make a reply. Some archaeological writers like this treatment; others find it too adversarial. Certainly it can give you some idea of what others think of your work. There are also various citation indexes that can indicate how much interest has been shown in a paper within the archaeological and related professions, although references to the paper might have been negative rather than positive. I recently confessed to a German colleague that I had never looked myself up in a citation index, as I am told many younger writers do. His response was an emphatic insistence that neither had he.

In the end, however, it is the readers' reception of a publication that is most important. This can be difficult to ascertain. Occasionally, kind colleagues will write to you to say how much they enjoyed your book or paper; sometimes requests might arrive from the most unlikely places asking for an offprint or photocopy or PDF of a paper. I even had one correspondent who sent me three pages of closely written notes about the things I could have done better in one of my publications. Perhaps one's colleagues or the institution to which one is affiliated will show approval by organizing a book launch. However, these things represent a very limited readership and probably few sales. For many books, a publisher will be looking for sales in the thousands rather than the hundreds. The extent to which this is achieved will depend not only on the quality of a publication but also on the effectiveness of the publishers' advertising and distribution network. I have known of books where the publishers have handled these matters so inadequately that many potential purchasers have not even known that a book existed until it came to their notice by accident. Formerly, booksellers could also help to get books into readers' hands, but many of their shops have now degenerated into markets for pulp fiction, as specialist publications have increasingly been sold online. However, the Internet does help to inform people about recent books and even provides access to journal papers that otherwise would only be available to relatively few individuals or institutions. Nevertheless, the readership of such papers is often small. There is the old story about an academic who complained to a colleague that he doubted whether more than ten people ever read his papers, to which his colleague answered that this was good because only about five people read his.

The extent to which a book is bought, by either individuals or libraries, will depend on many factors, of which price can be important. It will vary from hardback to paperback to digital editions, and if a publisher decides to produce only a hardback version the cost can be prohibitive, even for some libraries. Needless to say, the author has no control over price, except that the size and complexity of the book that she or he writes will obviously have an impact on it. Sales will also be affected by the extent to which university teachers of archaeology recommend a book to students, even if it was not actually written as a textbook. In addition, the subject of a book is important; as mentioned in Chapter 7, topics such as Egyptology, Greek and Roman archaeology and ancient China attract a wide readership amongst the general public. In contrast, the later archaeology of Africa, for example, excites little interest. Nevertheless, publishers continue to produce numerous specialized archaeological texts that must inevitably have limited sales. I once asked the commissioning editor for archaeology at a major international publisher how it could afford to produce some of the more esoteric archaeological books. Years later I am still pondering whether the answer I got was a compliment or an insult. 'We can afford to publish books of that sort', I was told, 'because we also publish books by people like you.'

I have been told that the print run for many books about archaeology will often be only 1,000 to 1,500 copies, although for more 'popular' publications it is no doubt larger. If the sales of a book are good, perhaps because it has attracted the interest of a wider range of readers than was expected, a publisher might decide to reprint it, and maybe another 1,000 copies will be produced. This can happen without consultation with the author, who in many instances might not even know that it has occurred. Indeed, publishers often show little interest in keeping the author informed about the progress of sales, although these can be ascertained from the periodic royalty statements if the publication is one that earns royalties. As time goes on and if the book continues to sell at an acceptable rate or there is a continuing demand for it after it has gone out of print, further reprints might appear, usually without revision. For example, one of my books was reprinted twenty-eight years after its original publication (Connah 2009). Continued reprinting will eventually cause the author to become concerned about the book going out of date. In such instances, authors might console themselves with the fact that this begins to happen even between submission and publication, but the time might come when a second edition of the book is clearly needed. The author will often be more concerned about this than the publisher, who might be reluctant to publish a new edition while reprints of the previous one are still selling. Even when it is conceded that a new edition is needed, publishers will often tell an author that the book can be revised to bring it up to date but that it must not increase in length or in number of illustrations. In practice this can prove difficult without the book being reset, which will allow more radical changes to be incorporated if the publishers agree. For the author, however, a second or third or even later edition is likely to prove increasingly difficult as one continually attempts to revise a book written years before. If one were to write it now, it would be written in a different way. The only answer might be to rewrite the book completely, and sometimes this does happen, occasionally with a different title. Not surprisingly, however, there are instances when an author declines an invitation to prepare a new edition or when another author or authors take over the work.

Such are the penalties of success, but what happens if a book does not sell? If sales are poor or very slow, a publisher will eventually decide that storage costs are exceeding income and will either offer the book at a reduced price or sell the stock into the remainder trade. Thus it is that booksellers' catalogues can sometimes advertise publications at a fraction of their original recommended retail price. Experienced book buyers know that such material contains a lot of junk, books that are inaccurate, superficial or just badly written, but they also know that there will be some good and important books there as well. In fact, books that are remaindered are not necessarily bad books; some of the most able of archaeological authors have had some of their efforts finish up amongst the bargains. One needs to be philosophical about such things; to be any sort of an author takes writing ability and confidence, but to be an archaeological author can also require both courage and determination.

In conclusion, it is essential that the archaeological author grasps the main idea that has been pursued in this book: to write about archaeology we need to know our archaeology but we also need to know how to write. The only way to learn this is to write and write and write. Each one of us must discover our own best way to do it; the purpose of this book has not been to present a prescriptive formula for success but to persuade each author to think about writing and to seek to understand the process of writing and publication. Eventually, with continued practice and thoughtful introspection we might even learn to write well; it is just as important to achieve this, as it is to excavate well or to adopt the latest analytical methods and theoretical ideas. Our archaeological achievements will not exist unless we can present them to the world, and we need to be able to accomplish this in an understandable, engaging and logically structured written form. In the end, archaeology is a literary discipline.

References

ADS 2008. 'Archaeology Data Service', http://ads.ahds.ac.uk/ Accessed 25 August 2008.

Alcock, S. E. and Osborne, R. (eds.) 2007. *Classical archaeology*. Oxford: Blackwell.

Allen, R. E. (ed.) 1990. *The concise Oxford dictionary of current English*. Oxford: Clarendon Press.

Andah, B. W., de Maret, P. and Soper, R. (eds.) 1993. *Proceedings of the 9th Congress of the Pan-African Association of Pre-history and Related Studies: Jos, 11–17 December 1983*. Ibadan: Rex Charles.

Antiquaries Journal 2008. 'Guidance for *Journal* contributors', *Antiquaries Journal* 88: inside back cover.

Antiquaries Journal 2009. 'Notes for contributors', www.sal.org.uk/ books/theantiquariesjournal/notesforjournalcontributors/ Accessed 19 February 2009.

Atkinson, R. J. C. 1953. *Field archaeology*. Second Edition. London: Methuen.

Bacon, F. 1909 [1597]. *Essays civil and moral*. London: Cassell.

Bahn, P. 1989. *Bluff your way in archaeology*. Horsham, West Sussex: Ravette.

Bahn, P. 2007. 'Hunting for clues in the Palaeolithic', *Antiquity* **81**: 1086–8.

Bateman, T. 1861. *Ten years' diggings in Celtic and Saxon grave hills, in the counties of Derby, Stafford, and York, from 1848 to 1858 ...* London: J. R. Smith and Derby: W. Bemrose & Sons.

Belzoni, G. 1971 [1820]. *Narrative of the operations and recent discoveries within the pyramids, temples, tombs, and excavations, in Egypt and Nubia.* Farnborough, Hants, England: Gregg International.

Bentley, R. A. 2006. 'Academic copying, archaeology and the English language', *Antiquity* **80**: 196–201.

Bentley, R. A. and Maschner, H. D. G. 2008. 'Introduction: On archaeological theories', in *Handbook of archaeological theories*, eds. R. A. Bentley, H. D. G. Maschner and C. Chippindale, pp. 1–8. Lanham, MD: AltaMira.

Beresford, M. W. and St Joseph, J. K. S. 1979. *Medieval England: An aerial survey.* Second Edition. Cambridge: Cambridge University Press.

Berger, S., Feldner, H. and Passmore, K. 2003. *Writing history: Theory and practice.* London: Arnold.

Betty, P. K. 2002. 'Anyone for writing?' *Antiquity* **76**: 1054–8.

Binford, L. R. 1962. 'Archaeology as anthropology', *American Antiquity* **28**(2): 217–25.

Binford, L. R. 1988. *In pursuit of the past: Decoding the archaeological record.* London: Thames and Hudson. First published 1983.

Bintliff, J. 2008. 'History and continental approaches', in *Handbook of archaeological theories*, eds. R. A. Bentley, H. D. G. Maschner and C. Chippindale, pp. 147–64. Lanham, MD: AltaMira.

Bohrer, S. P. and Connah, G. E. 1971. 'Pathology in 700-year-old Nigerian bones. Query: sickle cell infarcts', *Radiology* **98**(3): 581–4.

Borghoff, U. M., Rödig, P., Scheffczyk, J. and Schmitz, L. 2005. *Long-term preservation of digital documents: Principles and practices.* Berlin: Springer-Verlag. First published 2003 in German.

Braidwood, R. J. 1981. 'Archaeological retrospect 2', *Antiquity* **55**: 19–26.

Branigan, K. 1974. *Reconstructing the past: A basic introduction to archaeology.* Newton Abbot: David and Charles.

Brassington, M. 1971. 'A Trajanic kiln complex near Little Chester, Derby, 1968', *Antiquaries Journal* **51**(1): 36–69.

Breunig, P., Garba, A. and Hambolu, M. 2001. 'From ceramics to culture: Studies in the Final Stone Age Gajiganna Complex of NE-Nigeria', Frankfurt am Main: *Berichte des Sonderforschungsbereichs 268*, Band **14**, pp. 45–53.

Brindley, L. 2009. 'We're in danger of losing our memories', *The Observer*, UK, 25 January.

Brodribb, C. 1970. *Drawing archaeological finds for publication.* London: John Baker.

Brown, A. 2006. *Archiving websites: A practical guide for information management professionals.* London: Facet Publishing.

Bruce-Mitford, R. L. S. 1968. 'Sutton Hoo excavations, 1965–7', *Antiquity* 42: 36–9 and Frontispiece and Plates VI and VII.

Bulleid, A. H. 1958. *The lake-villages of Somerset.* Fifth Edition. Wells and London: Clare, Son and Company.

Bulleid, A. H. and Gray, H. St G. 1911 and 1917. *The Glastonbury Lake Village: A full description of the excavations and the relics discovered 1892–1907.* Volumes I and II. Taunton: Glastonbury Antiquarian Society, Wessex Press.

Butcher, J. 1981. *Copy-editing: The Cambridge handbook.* Second Edition. Cambridge: Cambridge University Press.

Caneva, I. 1991. 'Jebel Moya revisited: A settlement of the 5th millennium BC in the middle Nile Basin', *Antiquity* 65: 262–8.

Carey, G. V. 1960. *Mind the stop: A brief guide to punctuation with a note on proof-correction.* Second Edition. Cambridge: Cambridge University Press.

Carr, E. H. 1961. *What is history? The George Macaulay Trevelyan Lectures delivered in the University of Cambridge January–March 1961.* London: Macmillan.

Carver, M. 2006. 'Editorial', *Antiquity* 80: 517–22.

Caton-Thompson, G. 1931. *The Zimbabwe culture: Ruins and reactions.* Oxford: Clarendon Press.

Chamberlain, A. F. 1907. 'Thomas Jefferson's ethnological opinions and activities', *American Anthropologist* (New Series) 9(3): 499–509.

Champion, S. and Chippindale, C. (eds.) 1997. 'Special review section: Electronic Archaeology', *Antiquity* 71: 1026–76.

Cherry, J. F. and Torrence, R. (eds.) 1988. 'Editorial note', in L. R. Binford, *In pursuit of the past: Decoding the archaeological record*, pp. 9–11. London: Thames and Hudson. First published 1983.

Childe, V. G. 1927. *The dawn of European civilization.* Second Edition. London: Kegan Paul, Trench, Trubner & Co.

Childe, V. G. 1931. 'Skara Brae: A "Stone Age" village in Orkney', *Antiquity* 5: 47–59.

Chippindale, C. 1989. '"Social archaeology" in the nineteenth century: Is it right to look for modern ideas in old places?' in *Tracing archaeology's past: The historiography of archaeology*, ed. A. L. Christenson, pp. 21–33. Carbondale and Edwardsville: Southern Illinois University Press.

Chippindale, C. 1996. 'On writing about archaeology in the English language', *Archaeological Dialogues* 1: 47–55.

Clark, [J.] G. [D.] 1944–1945. *Prehistoric England*. Third Edition. London: Batsford. First published 1940.

Clark, J. G. D. 1952. *Prehistoric Europe: The economic basis*. London: Methuen.

Clark, [J.] G. [D.] 1957. *Archaeology and society: Reconstructing the prehistoric past*. Third Edition. London: Methuen. First published 1939.

Clark, [J.] G. [D.] 1961. *World prehistory: An outline*. Cambridge: Cambridge University Press.

Clark, [J.] G. [D.] 1969. *World prehistory: A new outline: Being the second edition of 'World prehistory'*. Cambridge: Cambridge University Press.

Clark, [J.] G. [D.] 1977. *World prehistory: In new perspective: An illustrated third edition*. Cambridge: Cambridge University Press.

Clarke, D. L. 1972a. 'A provisional model of an Iron Age society and its settlement system', in *Models in archaeology*, ed. D. L. Clarke, pp. 801–69. London: Methuen.

Clarke, D. L. 1972b. 'Models and paradigms in contemporary archaeology', in *Models in archaeology*, ed. D. L. Clarke, pp. 1–60. London: Methuen.

Clarke, D. L. and Connah, G. 1962. 'Remanent magnetism and beaker chronology', *Antiquity* **36**: 206–9.

Coles, J. and Orme, B. 1976. 'A Neolithic hurdle from the Somerset Levels', *Antiquity* **50**: 57–60 and Plate VIII.

Collins Persse, M. D. de B. 1981. 'Fairbairn, Stephen (1862–1938)', *Australian dictionary of biography*, Volume **8**. Melbourne: Melbourne University Press, pp. 459–60. http://www.adb.online.anu.edu.au/biogs/A080484b.htm Accessed 3 June 2008.

Conlon, V. M. 1973. *Camera techniques in archaeology*. London: John Baker.

Connah, G. 1954. 'Bromborough water mill', *Bromborough Society Twenty-First Annual Report and Balance Sheet 1953–1954*: no pagination (8 pages).

Connah, G. 1962. 'An archaeological experiment with the "4c" mine detector', *Antiquity* **36**: 305–6.

Connah, G. (asst. ed.) 1971–1973. *West African Journal of Archaeology* **1–3**.

Connah, G. 1975. *The archaeology of Benin: Excavations and other researches in and around Benin City, Nigeria*. Oxford: Clarendon Press.

Connah, G. 1981a. *Three thousand years in Africa: Man and his environment in the Lake Chad region of Nigeria*. Cambridge: Cambridge University Press.

Connah, G. 1981b. 'Man and a lake', in *2000 ans d'histoire africaine: Le sol, la parole et l'écrit: Mélanges en hommage à Raymond Mauny*, Tome I, pp. 161–78. Paris: Société française d'histoire d'outre-mer.

Connah, G. (ed.) 1983. *Australian field archaeology: A guide to techniques*. Canberra: Australian Institute of Aboriginal Studies.

Connah, G. (ed.) 1983–1988. *Australian Journal of Historical Archaeology* 1–6.

Connah, G. 1987. *African civilizations: Precolonial cities and states in tropical Africa: An archaeological perspective*. Cambridge: Cambridge University Press.

Connah, G. 1988. *'Of the hut I builded': The archaeology of Australia's history*. Melbourne: Cambridge University Press.

Connah, G. 1993a. Japanese edition of Connah 1987. Tokyo: Kawade Shobo.

Connah, G. 1993b. *The archaeology of Australia's history*. Melbourne: Cambridge University Press. (Paperback edition of Connah 1988.)

Connah, G. 1996a. *Kibiro: The salt of Bunyoro, past and present*. London: British Institute in Eastern Africa.

Connah, G. (ed.) 1996b [dated 1995]. *Australasian Historical Archaeology* 12.

Connah, G. (ed.) 1997. *The archaeology of Lake Innes House: Investigating the visible evidence 1993–1995*. Canberra: Connah for the New South Wales National Parks and Wildlife Service.

Connah, G. (ed.) 1998. *Transformations in Africa: Essays on Africa's later past*. London: Leicester University Press (Cassell Academic).

Connah, G. 2001a. *African civilizations: An archaeological perspective*. Second Edition. Cambridge: Cambridge University Press.

Connah, G. 2001b. 'Writing Africa's archaeological past: Who writes for whom?' *Australasian Review of African Studies* 23(1): 32–7.

Connah, G. 2004a. *Forgotten Africa: An introduction to its archaeology*. London and New York: Routledge.

Connah, G. 2004b. 'Publish and be damned?' in *Fifty years in the archaeology of Africa: Themes in archaeological theory and practice. Papers in honour of John Alexander*, eds. L. Smith, P. Rose, G. Wahida, and S. Wahida. *Azania* Special Volume 39: 325–36.

Connah, G. 2004c. 'Writing Africa's archaeological past', *Nyame Akuma* 62: 78–80.

Connah, G. 2006. *Unbekanntes Afrika: Archäologische Entdeckungen auf dem schwarzen Kontinent*. Übersetzung aus dem Englischen von

Beate Dillmann-Gräsing. Stuttgart: Konrad Theiss. (German edition of Connah 2004a.)

Connah, G. 2007. *The same under a different sky? A country estate in nineteenth-century New South Wales.* Oxford: British Archaeological Reports, International Series **1625**.

Connah, G. 2008. *Afrique oubliée: Une introduction à l'archéologie du continent.* Traduit de l'anglais par Anne Haour et Céline Moguen. Paris: L'Harmattan. (French edition of Connah 2004a.)

Connah, G. 2009. *Three thousand years in Africa: Man and his environment in the Lake Chad region of Nigeria.* Cambridge: Cambridge University Press. (Paperback edition of Connah 1981a.)

Connah, G., Rowland, M. J. and Oppenheimer, J. 1978. *Captain Richards' house at Winterbourne: A study in historical archaeology.* Armidale: University of New England.

Cookson, M. B. 1954. *Photography for archaeologists.* London: Parrish.

Copeland, R. 1998. *Blue and white transfer-printed pottery.* Princes Risborough: Shire Publications.

Crook, J. 1991. 'The Pilgrims' Hall, Winchester: Hammerbeams, base crucks and aisle-derivative roof structures', *Archaeologia* **109**: 129–59.

Cunliffe, B. 1971. 'Danebury, Hampshire: First interim report on the excavation, 1969–70', *Antiquaries Journal* **51**(2): 240–52.

Cunliffe, B, 1972. 'Excavations at Portchester Castle, Hants, 1969–1971: Fourth interim report', *Antiquaries Journal* **52**(1): 70–83.

Current Archaeology 2008. http://www.archaeology.co.uk/Home Page. Accessed 2 May 2008.

Daniel, G. E. 1943. *The three ages: An essay in archaeological method.* Cambridge: Cambridge University Press.

Daniel, G. [E.] 1959. 'Stonehenge restored', *Antiquity* **33**: 50–1 and Frontispiece.

Daniel, G. [E.] 1967. *The origins and growth of archaeology.* Harmondsworth: Penguin.

Daniel, G. [E.] 1975. *A hundred and fifty years of archaeology.* London: Duckworth.

Daniel, G. [E.] 1976. *Cambridge and the back-looking curiosity: An inaugural lecture.* Cambridge: Cambridge University Press.

Deetz, J. 1977. *In small things forgotten: The archaeology of early American life.* Garden City, New York: Anchor Books.

Deetz, J. 1988. 'History and archaeological theory: Walter Taylor revisited', *American Antiquity* **53**(1): 13–22.

Derricourt, R. 1996a. *An author's guide to scholarly publishing.* Princeton, New Jersey: Princeton University Press.

Derricourt, R. 1996b. *Ideas into books: A guide to scholarly and non-fiction publishing*. Ringwood, Victoria: Penguin Books (Australian edition of Derricourt 1996a).

Deuel, L. 1969. *Flights into yesterday: The story of aerial archaeology*. Harmondsworth: Penguin.

Dorrell, P. G. 1989. *Photography in archaeology and conservation*. Cambridge: Cambridge University Press.

Dowson, T. A. 1993. 'Changing fortunes of Southern African archaeology: Comment on A. D. Mazel's "history"', *Antiquity* 67: 641–4.

Duckers, P. 2000. *British campaign medals 1815–1914*. Princes Risborough: Shire Publications.

Eriksen, T. H. 2005. 'Nothing to lose but our aitches', *Anthropology Today* 21(2): 1–2.

Fagan, B. M. 1959. 'Cropmarks in antiquity', *Antiquity* 33: 279–81.

Fagan, B. M. 1975. *The rape of the Nile: Tomb robbers, tourists, and archaeologists in Egypt*. New York: Charles Scribners.

Fagan, B. M. 1978. 'Gundu and Ndonde, Basanga and Mwanamaimpa', *Azania* 13: 127–34.

Fagan, B. M. 1983. *People of the Earth: An introduction to world prehistory*. Fourth Edition. Boston: Little, Brown.

Fagan, B. M. 2004. *The long summer: How climate changed civilization*. London: Granta Books.

Fagan, B. M. 2006a. *Writing archaeology: Telling stories about the past*. Walnut Creek, CA: Left Coast Press.

Fagan, B. M. 2006b. *Fish on Friday: Feasting, fasting, and the discovery of the New World*. New York: Basic Books.

Fagan, B. M. 1974–2007. *Men of the earth: An introduction to world prehistory*. First Edition. Boston: Little, Brown. Subsequently titled *People of the earth: An introduction to world prehistory*. Second to Twelfth Edition. Latterly Upper Saddle River, NJ: Pearson Prentice Hall.

Fisher, C. L., Reinhard, K. J., Kirk, M. and DiVirgilio, J. 2007. 'Privies and parasites: The archaeology of health conditions in Albany, New York', *Historical Archaeology* 41(4): 172–97.

Flannery, K. V. 1976. 'Research strategy and Formative Mesoamerica', in *The early Mesoamerican village*, ed. K. V. Flannery, pp. 1–11. New York: Academic Press.

Flannery, K. V. 1982. 'The golden Marshalltown: A parable for the archeology of the 1980s', *American Anthropologist (New Series)* 84(2): 265–78.

Fowler, H. W. 1965. *A dictionary of modern English usage*. Second Edition, revised by E. Gowers. Oxford: Clarendon Press.

Fowler, H. W. and Fowler, F. G. 1962. *The King's English*. Third Edition. Oxford: Clarendon Press.

Fox, A. 1972. 'The Holcombe mirror', *Antiquity* **46**: 293–6 and Plates XLIV and XLV.

Fox, A. L. 1875. 'On early modes of navigation', *Journal of the Anthropological Institute of Great Britain and Ireland* **4**: 399–437.

Frere, J. 1800. 'Account of flint weapons discovered at Hoxne in Suffolk', *Archaeologia* **XIII**: 204–5 and Plates XIV and XV.

Garlake, P. S. 1973. *Great Zimbabwe*. New York: Stein and Day.

Gosden, C. 1992. 'Endemic doubt: Is what we write right?' *Antiquity* **66**: 803–8.

Grafton, A. 2007. *What was history? The art of history in early modern Europe*. Cambridge: Cambridge University Press.

Griffiths, N., Jenner, A. and Wilson, C. 1990. *Drawing archaeological finds: A handbook*. London: Occasional Paper No.13, Institute of Archaeology, University College London.

Grinsell, L., Rahtz, P. and Warhurst, A. 1966. *The preparation of archaeological reports*. London: John Baker.

Grøn, O. 2003. 'Mesolithic dwelling places in south Scandinavia: Their definition and social interpretation', *Antiquity* **77**: 685–708.

Hall, R. 2007. *Exploring the world of the Vikings*. London: Thames and Hudson.

Harding, D. W. and Blake, I. M. 1963. 'An Early Iron Age settlement in Dorset', *Antiquity* **37**: 63–4 and Plate VIII.

Harp, E. Jr (ed.) 1975. *Photography in archaeological research*. Albuquerque: University of New Mexico Press.

Harvey, R. 2005. *Preserving digital materials*. München: Saur Verlag.

Hawkes, J. 1982. *Mortimer Wheeler: Adventurer in archaeology*. London: Weidenfeld and Nicolson.

Hendrickx, M. 2008. Letter to the *Sydney Morning Herald*, 14 November, p. 10.

Higgs, E. S. (ed.) 1972. *Papers in economic prehistory: Studies by members and associates of the British Academy Major Research Project in the Early History of Agriculture*. Cambridge: Cambridge University Press.

Higgs, E. S. (ed.) 1975. *Palaeoeconomy: Being the second volume of papers in economic prehistory by members and associates of the British Academy Major Research Project in the Early History of Agriculture*. Cambridge: Cambridge University Press.

Hill, J. D., Spence, A. J., La Niece, S. and Worrell, S. 2004. 'The Winchester Hoard: A find of unique Iron Age gold jewellery from southern England', *Antiquaries Journal* **84**: 1–22.

Hiscock, P. 2008. *Archaeology of ancient Australia*. London: Routledge.

Hodder, I. 1989. 'Writing archaeology: Site reports in context', *Antiquity* 63: 268–74.

Hodder, I. 1991. 'Archaeological theory in contemporary European societies: The emergence of competing traditions', in *Archaeological theory in Europe: The last three decades*, ed. I. Hodder, pp. 1–24. London: Routledge.

Hope-Taylor, B. 1966. 'Archaeological draughtsmanship: Principles and practice. Part II: Ends and means', *Antiquity* 40: 107–13.

Hope-Taylor, B. 1967. 'Archaeological draughtsmanship: Principles and practice. Part III: Lines of communication', *Antiquity* 41: 181–9.

Howell, C. L. and Blanc, W. 1992. *A practical guide to archaeological photography*. Los Angeles: Institute of Archaeology, University of California Los Angeles.

Hummler, M. 2007. 'Review: New book chronicle', *Antiquity* 81: 1118–29.

Hunt, J. 2004. 'Sculpture, dates and patrons: Dating the Herefordshire School of Sculpture', *Antiquaries Journal* 84: 185–222.

Hunter, M. 1975. *John Aubrey and the realm of learning*. London: Duckworth.

Illustrated London News 1911. 'Not the woad-daubed savage of the old history-books: The civilised ancient Briton: The lake village near Glastonbury', 2 December: pp. 928–33.

Internet Archaeology 2008. http://intarch.ac.uk Accessed 27 April 2008.

Jones, S., MacSween, A., Jeffrey, S., Morris, R. and Heyworth, M. 2001. *From the ground up: The publication of archaeological projects. A user needs survey*. Council for British Archaeology. http://www.britarch.ac.uk/pubs/puns/index.html Accessed 19 December 2007.

Joyce, R.[A.] 2006. 'Writing historical archaeology', in *The Cambridge companion to historical archaeology*, eds. D. Hicks and M. C. Beaudry, pp. 48–65. Cambridge: Cambridge University Press.

Joyce, R. A., Guyer, C., Joyce, M., Lopiparo, J. and Preucel, R. 2002. *The languages of archaeology: Dialogue, narrative, and writing*. Oxford: Blackwell.

Kirkpatrick, B. 1998. *Roget's thesaurus*. New Edition. London: Penguin Books.

Kitchen, K. A. 1998. 'The curse of publication and the blight of novelty', in *Proceedings of the Seventh International Congress of Egyptologists: Cambridge 3–9 September 1995*, ed. C. J. Eyre, pp. 625–30. Leuven: Uitgeverij Peeters.

Klindt-Jensen, O. 1959. 'The Gundestrup Bowl: A reassessment', *Antiquity* 33: 161–9 and Plates XVII–XX.

Kuzmin, Y. V. 2006. 'Chronology of the earliest pottery in East Asia: Progress and pitfalls', *Antiquity* 80: 362–71.

Lal, B. B. 1972. 'The Copper Hoard culture of the Ganga Valley', *Antiquity* **46**: 282–7 and Plates XLb–XLIII.

Landes, K. K. 1966. 'A scrutiny of the abstract, II', *Bulletin of the American Association of Petroleum Geologists* **50**(9): 1992.

Layard, A. H. 1853. *Discoveries in the ruins of Nineveh and Babylon*. London: John Murray.

Lejju, B. J., Robertshaw, P. and Taylor, D. 2006. 'Africa's earliest bananas?' *Journal of Archaeological Science* **33**: 102–13.

Lloyd, S. 1955. *Foundations in the dust: A story of Mesopotamian exploration*. Harmondsworth: Penguin.

Lubbock, J. 1869. *Pre-historic times, as illustrated by ancient remains and the manners and customs of modern savages*. Second Edition. London: Williams and Norgate.

Luey, B. 2002. *Handbook for academic authors*. Fourth Edition. Cambridge: Cambridge University Press.

Lyon, E. A. 1989. 'A documentation strategy for archaeology', in *Tracing archaeology's past: The historiography of archaeology*, ed. A. L Christenson, pp. 187–98. Carbondale and Edwardsville: Southern Illinois University Press.

Lyons, T. R. and Avery, T. E. 1977. *Remote sensing: A handbook for archeologists and cultural resource managers*. Washington, DC: Cultural Resources Management Division, National Park Service, US Department of the Interior.

McIntosh, R. J. 1998. *The peoples of the Middle Niger: The Island of Gold*. Oxford: Blackwell.

Marsden, B. M. 2007. *The Barrow Knight: A life of Thomas Bateman, archaeologist and collector (1821–1861)*. Chesterfield, Derbyshire, UK: Bannister Publications.

Marsden, P. 1972. 'Archaeology at sea', *Antiquity* **46**: 198–202 and Plates XXV–XXVIII.

Masanès, J. 2006. *Web archiving*. Berlin: Springer-Verlag.

Maschner, H. D. G. 1991. 'The emergence of cultural complexity on the northern Northwest Coast', *Antiquity* **65**: 924–34.

Matthews, J. R., Bowen, J. M. and Matthews, R. W. 2000. *Successful scientific writing: A step-by-step guide for the biological and medical sciences*. Second Edition. Cambridge: Cambridge University Press.

Mégaloudi, F., Papadopoulos, S. and Sgourou, M. 2007. 'Plant offerings from the classical necropolis of Limenas, Thasos, northern Greece', *Antiquity* **81**: 933–43.

Merriam-Webster 2001. *Merriam-Webster's collegiate dictionary*. Tenth Edition. Springfield, MA: Merriam-Webster.

Metric system 2008. http://en.wikipedia.org/wiki/Metric_system Accessed 8 June 2008.

Mitchell, P. 2005. *African connections: An archaeological perspective on Africa and the wider world*. Walnut Creek, CA: AltaMira.

Mumford, W. 1983. 'Stone artefacts – an illustrator's primer', in *Australian field archaeology: A guide to techniques*, ed. G. Connah, pp. 160–8. Canberra: Australian Institute of Aboriginal Studies.

Mytum, H. C. 1978. 'Microfiche: a solution to the publication crisis?' *Antiquity* 52: 43–4.

Oakes, C. M. and Costen, M. 2003. 'The Congresbury carvings – an eleventh-century saint's shrine?' *Antiquaries Journal* 83: 281–309.

OASIS 2008. Online AccesS to the Index of archaeological investigationS. http://oasis.ac.uk/ Accessed 25 August 2008.

Orwell, G. 1946. 'Politics and the English language', in *The collected essays, journalism and letters of George Orwell*, eds. S. Orwell and I. Angus, 1971–1975, Volume 4: *In front of your nose, 1945–1950*, pp. 156–70. Harmondsworth: Penguin.

Osland, D., Boyd, D., McKenna, W. and Salusinszky, I. 1991. *Writing in Australia: A composition course for tertiary students*. Sydney: Harcourt Brace Jovanovich.

Owen, T. D. and Steele, J. N. 2001. *Digging up the past: Archaeology for kids*. Blackwood, South Australia: Southern Archaeology.

Parker, A. J. 1990. 'Classical antiquity: The maritime dimension', *Antiquity* 64: 335–46.

Pearson, D. and Webb, C. 2008. 'Defining file format obsolescence: A risky journey', *International Journal of Digital Curation* 3(1): 89–106.

Peden, W. (ed.) 1955. *Notes on the State of Virginia* by Thomas Jefferson, 1787. Chapel Hill: University of North Carolina Press.

Petrie, W. M. F. 1894. *A history of Egypt: Volume I: From the earliest times to the XVI Dynasty*. London: Methuen.

Phillips, J. E. 2005. '"To make the dry bones live": Amédée Forestier's Glastonbury Lake Village', in *Envisioning the past: Archaeology and the image*, eds. S. Smiles and S. Moser, pp. 72–91. Oxford: Blackwell.

Piggott, S. 1950. *William Stukeley: An eighteenth-century antiquary*. Oxford: Clarendon Press.

Piggott, S. 1954. *The Neolithic cultures of the British Isles: A study of the stone-using agricultural communities of Britain in the second millennium B.C.* Cambridge: Cambridge University Press.

Piggott, S. 1958. 'The excavation of the West Kennet Long Barrow: 1955–6', *Antiquity* 32: 235–42 and Plate XXV.

Piggott, S. 1965. 'Archaeological draughtsmanship: Principles and practice. Part I: Principles and retrospect', *Antiquity* 39: 165–76.

Pitt Rivers, Lieutenant-General. 1892. *Excavations in Bokerly and Wansdyke, Dorset and Wilts. 1888–1891.* Volume **III**. London: Privately printed.

Pitt Rivers, Lieutenant-General. 1898. *Excavations at Cranborne Chase, near Rushmore... 1893–1896.* Volume **IV**. London: Privately printed.

Pluciennik, M. 1999. 'Archaeological narratives and other ways of telling', *Current Anthropology* **40**(5): 653–78.

PPS 1982–1989. *Proceedings of the Prehistoric Society* **48–55**.

Prummel, W., Niekus, M. J. L.Th., van Gijn, A. L. and Cappers, R. T. J. 2002. 'A Late Mesolithic kill site of aurochs at Jardinga, Netherlands', *Antiquity* **76**: 413–24.

'Publish, not perish: The art and craft of publishing in scientific journals' 2008, University of Colorado libraries. http://www.publishnotperish.org/intro/ Accessed 25 August 2008.

Pwiti, G. and Soper, R. (eds.) 1996. *Aspects of African archaeology: Papers from the 10th Congress of the PanAfrican Association for Prehistory and Related Studies.* Harare: University of Zimbabwe.

Reade, J. 1998. 'Layard's *Nineveh and its remains.*' *Antiquity* **72**: 913–16.

Reid, A. M. and Lane, P. J. 2004. 'African historical archaeologies: An introductory consideration of scope and potential', in *African historical archaeologies*, eds. A. M. Reid and P. J. Lane, pp. 1–32. New York: Kluwer Academic/Plenum Publishers.

Renfrew, C. 1982. *Towards an archaeology of mind: An inaugural lecture delivered before the University of Cambridge on 30 November 1982.* Cambridge: Cambridge University Press.

Renn, D. F. 1959. 'Mottes: A classification', *Antiquity* **33**: 106–12.

Richter, I. A. (ed.) 1952. *Selections from the notebooks of Leonardo da Vinci.* London: The World's Classics, Oxford University Press.

Ritter, R. M. (ed.) 2003. *The Oxford style manual.* Oxford: Oxford University Press.

Robertshaw, P. 2006. 'Africa's earliest bananas: A new discovery peels back the history of our favorite fruit', *Archaeology* **59**(5): 25–9.

Rodden, R. J. 1962. 'Excavations at the Early Neolithic site at Nea Nikomedeia, Greek Macedonia (1961 season)', *Proceedings of the Prehistoric Society* (New Series) **28**: 267–88.

Roth, H. L. 1903. *Great Benin: Its customs, art and horrors.* Reissued 1968. London: Routledge & Kegan Paul.

Scarre, C. (ed.) 2005. *The human past: World prehistory and the development of human societies.* London: Thames and Hudson.

Schrire, C. 1995. *Digging through darkness: Chronicles of an archaeologist.* Charlottesville and London: University Press of Virginia.

Shanks, M. 2004. 'Three rooms: Archaeology and performance', *Journal of Social Archaeology* **4**(2): 147–80.

Shanks, M. 2008. 'Post-processual archaeology and after', in *Handbook of archaeological theories*, eds. R. A. Bentley, H. D. G. Maschner and C. Chippindale, pp. 133–44. Lanham, MD: AltaMira.

Shaw, T. 1961. *Excavation at Dawu: Report on an excavation in a mound at Dawu, Akuapim, Ghana*. Edinburgh: Thomas Nelson and Sons.

Shinnie, P. L. 1967. *Meroe: A civilization of the Sudan*. London: Thames and Hudson.

Silverberg, R. 1985. *Great adventures in archaeology*. Harmondsworth: Penguin.

Simmons, H. C. 1969. *Archaeological photography*. New York: New York University Press.

Sinclair, A. 1989. 'Writing ARC-haeology', *Archaeological Review from Cambridge* 8(2): 159–64.

Sisson, C. H. 1975. *The poetic art: A translation of Horace's Ars Poetica*. Cheadle, UK: Carcanet.

Smith, I. F. 1955. 'Bibliography of the publications of Professor V. Gordon Childe', *Proceedings of the Prehistoric Society* (New Series) 21: 295–304.

Smith, L., Rose, P., Wahida, G. and Wahida, S. (eds.) 2004. *Fifty years in the archaeology of Africa: Themes in archaeological theory and practice. Papers in honour of John Alexander. Azania* Special Volume 39.

Sorrell, A. 1981. *Reconstructing the past*. London: Batsford.

St Joseph, J. K. 1967. 'Air reconnaissance: Recent results, 11', *Antiquity* 41: 216–18 and Plate XXIV.

Strunk, W. Jr. and White, E. B. 2000. *The elements of style*. Fourth Edition. New York: Longman.

Style manual: For authors, editors and printers, 2002. Sixth Edition, 2007 Reprint. Canberra: John Wiley & Sons, Australia.

Taylor, W. W. 1948. *A study of archeology*. Washington, DC: American Anthropological Association, Memoir Number 69. (Cited by Joyce et al. 2002.)

Taylor, W. W. 1983. *A study of archeology*. Carbondale: Southern Illinois University Press.

Thompson, E. H. 1933. *People of the serpent: Life and adventure among the Mayas*. London: Putnam's Sons.

Thompson, M. W. 1977. *General Pitt-Rivers: Evolution and archaeology in the nineteenth century*. Bradford-on-Avon, Wiltshire: Moonraker Press.

Török, L. 1997. *Meroë City: An ancient African capital: John Garstang's excavations in the Sudan*, Parts 1 and 2. London: Egypt Exploration Society.

Trigger, B. G. 1978. *Time and traditions: Essays in archaeological interpretation.* Edinburgh: Edinburgh University Press.

Vatin, C. 1972. 'Wooden sculpture from Gallo-Roman Auvergne', *Antiquity* 46: 39–42 and Frontispiece, Backpiece, and Plates II–IX.

Watson, P. J. 1983. 'Foreword to the 1983 edition', in *A study of archaeology*, W. W. Taylor, 1983, pp. ix–xvi. Carbondale: Southern Illinois University Press.

Watson, P. J. 2008. 'Processualism and after', in *Handbook of archaeological theories*, eds. R. A. Bentley, H. D. G. Maschner and C. Chippindale, pp. 29–38. Lanham, MD: AltaMira.

Webster, G. S. 2008. 'Culture history: A culture-historical approach', in *Handbook of archaeological theories*, eds. R. A. Bentley, H. D. G. Maschner and C. Chippindale, pp. 11–27. Lanham, MD: AltaMira.

Webster, L. 2007. 'Review of H. Williams, 2006. *Death and memory in early medieval Britain.* Cambridge: Cambridge University Press.' *Antiquity* 81: 1115–16.

Wendt, K. P. 2007. *Gajiganna: Analysis of stratigraphies and pottery of a Final Stone Age culture of northeast Nigeria.* Frankfurt am Main: Africa Magna Verlag.

Wheeler, R. E. M. 1943. *Maiden Castle, Dorset.* London: Society of Antiquaries.

Wheeler, [R. E.] M. 1954. *Archaeology from the earth.* Oxford: Clarendon Press.

White [Schrire], C. 1971. 'Man and environment in northwest Arnhem Land', in *Aboriginal man and environment in Australia*, eds. D. J. Mulvaney and J. Golson, pp. 141–57. Canberra: Australian National University Press.

White, J. P. 1983. 'Report writing and publication', in *Australian field archaeology: A guide to techniques*, ed. G. Connah, pp. 171–8. Canberra: Australian Institute of Aboriginal Studies.

Willey, G. R. (ed.) 1988. *Excavations at Seibal, Department of Peten, Guatemala.* Cambridge, MA: Memoirs of the Peabody Museum of Archaeology and Ethnology, Harvard University, Volume 16.

Willey, G. R. and Sabloff, J. A. 1980. *A history of American archaeology.* Second Edition. San Francisco: Freeman and Company.

Woodbury, R. B. 1973. *Alfred V. Kidder.* New York and London: Columbia University Press.

Writing archaeology 1989. 'Issue theme', *Archaeological Review from Cambridge* 8(2): 159–231.

Yentsch, A. E. 1994. *A Chesapeake family and their slaves: A study in historical archaeology.* Cambridge: Cambridge University Press.

Yoffee, N. and Sherratt, A. 1993. 'Introduction: The sources of archaeological theory', in *Archaeological theory: Who sets the agenda?*, eds. N. Yoffee and A. Sherratt, pp. 1–9. Cambridge: Cambridge University Press.

Index

absolute dating, 63, 65
abstracts, 148–9, 162
abstracts in other languages,
   149
acknowledgements, 97, 151, 174
aerial photographs, 101, 179
agency theory, 61
American Antiquity, 54
Ancient Peoples and Places
   series, 155
Antiquaries Journal, 12, 93
Antiquity, 54, 104, 139
appendices, 141
archaeological 'canon,' 2
   consultants, 10, 46, 70, 138
   cultures, 63–4
   illustration, 13, 15, 19, 45–6,
      59–60, 91–135, 163, 173–4,
      176, 179–80

*Archaeological Method and
   Theory*, 58
archaeological theory, 33–5,
   60–62, 69–70
Archaeology, 56
Archaeology Data Service,
   139
Archaeometry, 55
archiving excavation records,
   141–2
'argument' approach, 76–7
assessment by colleagues and
   friends, 90
Atkinson, Richard, 92, 138
Aubrey, John, 13–14
author's affiliation, 150
author–editor relationship,
   165–7
author questionnaire, 181

author's writing, 2–3
authorship consistency, 150

'backwards timetable,' 84
Bacon, Francis, 72
Bahn, Paul, 62, 136
Bateman, Thomas, 18–19
Batsford, B.T., 166
Belzoni, Giovanni Battista, 17–18
bibliographies and lists of
    references, 88, 149–50, 162,
    178
Binford, Lewis R., 5, 33–4,
    66
Bintliff, J., 70
book 'flyers,' 182
    marketing, 181–2, 187–8
    prices, 187
    reviews, 56–7, 181, 185–6
    royalties, 97, 160, 188
    sales, 186–8
    sold online, 181, 187
bookshops, 181, 187
Boucher de Perthes, Jacques,
    19
brief 'life' of general syntheses,
    152
British Archaeological Reports,
    48, 182
British Institute in Eastern
    Africa, 48
British Library, 10
Brooks, Alasdair, 8

Camden, William, 12–14
captions, 179
    list, 101
    writing, 98–9
Cardano, Girolamo, 4
Carr, E.H., 60, 86
Carver, Martin, 104
Caton-Thompson, Gertrude,
    28–9

central themes, 152
Childe, Vere Gordon, 27–8, 63,
    97, 154
choosing a title, 74, 85, 180
citation indexes, 186
Clarendon (Oxford University
    Press), 160
Clark, Grahame, 32–3, 64–5, 105,
    166
Clarke, David L., 34–5, 47, 62,
    66
classical archaeologists, 67
cognitive archaeology, 38, 69
collaborative writing, 89, 151
commissioning editors, 159–61,
    163–4
communicating with readers, 35,
    44, 72, 74, 81, 96, 153–7
computer-generated
    line-drawings, 95, 104
Concise Oxford Dictionary of
    Current English, 9, 82
conference proceedings, 51–2,
    143–4
connectives, 78, 80
Cookson, M.B., 93
Copy-editing: The Cambridge
    Handbook, 175
copy editors, 90, 175–9
copyright fees, 97
    permissions, 96–7, 151, 174,
    182
cover, 180–81
culture-historical approach, 64,
    66
Current Archaeology, 55

daily word target, 84
Daniel, Glyn, 12–14, 63
da Vinci, Leonardo, 6
Deetz, James, 1, 8, 68
Derricourt, Robin, 8, 159, 173
difficulty of writing, 3, 86

digital publications, 9–10, 46–7,
 139, 141–2
technology, 94–5, 173
typesetting, 176–7
drawing accuracy, 96
dust jacket, 180–81

edited collections, 50–51, 136,
 143–4
editors, 158–71, 183, 185
ellipsis, 79
epochalism, 62–4
Evans, John, 19
expression, 81–82

Fagan, Brian M., 6–7, 37–8, 49,
 52, 68, 76, 84–5, 156
Fagan's 'hook,' 76, 85
Fairbairn, Steve, 73
festschrifts, 52
figures list, 101
finding a publisher, 159–61
first drafts, 85
first sentences, 85
Flannery, Kent V., 35–7, 66, 68
fold-outs, 137, 163
footnotes and endnotes, 88, 141,
 149, 162
Forestier, Amédée, 59–60
Frere, John, 14–15

general syntheses, 48–9, 151–5
Geographical Information
 Systems, 95
Glastonbury Lake-Village, 47,
 59–60
Gosden, C., 62
grey literature, 9–10, 46, 139

Handbook for Academic Authors,
 173
Harvard University, 48
headings and subheadings, 142–3

Hearne, Thomas, 14
Higgs, Eric, 66
Hodder, Ian, 7, 69
Horace (Roman writer), 90
house style, 99, 142, 144,
 175
Hume, Ivor Nöel, 8
hypothesis testing, 66

Illustrated London News, 59
illustration size, 100–101, 176,
 179
imagining the past, 60–2, 71
indexes, 162–3, 179–80
information for the editor or
 publisher, 100–102
instructions to contributors,
 143–4
integrating text and illustrations,
 97–100
International System of Units, 83

Jefferson, Thomas, 15–16
Journal of Archaeological Science,
 56
journal choice, 54–6, 143
editors, 55, 144, 166–8
'forums,' 186
keywords, 150
paper significance, 144–5
paper structure, 145
journals, 45–7, 53–7, 68, 143–51,
 166–70, 182–3, 186

Kidder, Alfred Vincent, 26–7, 64
Kossinna, Gustaf, 63

Layard, Austen Henry, 20–22
learning how to write, 3, 11, 58,
 68, 72, 146–7, 151–2, 189
Leland, John, 14
length of publications, 45, 55, 68,
 146–9, 162–3

line-drawings, 93–6, 104, 121–34, 163
literature about archaeological writing, 7–8
Lubbock, John, 19–20

maps, preparation of, 98
Marxism, 61
measurements, 83
Merriam-Webster's Collegiate Dictionary, 82
microfiche, 140, 142
minimizing monograph content, 140–2
miscellaneous publications, 46, 57–8
Mitchell, Peter, 39–40
models, 62
monographic excavation reports, 29, 47–8, 137–43
monographs, 47–53, 74–5, 136, 151–66
'mosaic' approach, 75
multiple authorship, 89, 151
Murray, Margaret, 23

'narrative' approach, 75–6
nature of archaeological evidence, 61–2, 66
New Archaeology, 11, 31, 33, 65, 68
non sequitur, 80
numbering illustrations, 99

OASIS project, 139
order of authorship, 89
Owen, Timothy, 157
Oxford Style Manual, 80, 173

PanAfrican Association for Prehistory and Related Studies, 51

paragraph sequence, length and continuity, 77–8
paragraph structure, 76–8
Penguin Books, 154
Petrie, William Matthew Flinders, 23–4, 47, 103
photographs, 93–4, 102–104, 106–20, 163
Piggott, Stuart, 92
Pitt Rivers, 2, 22, 47
popular interest in fantasy, 155
popularization, 57–8, 154–7
positioning figures and tables, 100
Posnansky, Merrick, 8
postmodernism, 62
post-processual archaeology, 38, 61, 69
Prehistoric Europe: The Economic Basis, 32, 64
Prelims (Preliminaries), 173
Prestwich, Joseph, 19
printing, 176
print-ready material, 182
print runs, 188
problems file, 87–8
Proceedings of the Prehistoric Society, 54
processual archaeology, 61, 66–7, 69
production team, 176
proof-correcting symbols, 178–9
proofs and proof-reading, 176–80
public interest in archaeology, 68, 154–7, 187
publication schedule, 175
publish or perish, 2
publishers, 44–5, 158–66, 171–2, 175, 186–9
    contracts, 160, 164–5
    proposal, 161–4

readers, 90, 160–61, 164, 168, 171
punctuation, 79–80

quantity and quality of illustrations, 102–104

readers' reactions, 186–7
reading, 6, 11–12, 146, 153
referees, 56, 90, 158, 168–70
referencing, 88, 149–50, 162, 178
Reisner, G.A., 26
remainders, 189
reprints and new editions, 188–9
review articles, 56, 185
revision, 50, 81, 85, 90, 148, 170, 188
Robertshaw, Peter, 55
Roget's *Thesaurus*, 80
running headlines, 179

Schrire, Carmel, 60
sentence continuity, 80
length, 18, 78–9
structure, 76, 78–9
Shanks, M., 69
Shaw, Thurstan, 6
Shire Books, 156
sic, 80
Sinclair, Anthony, 3
Society for Historical Archaeology, 6
specialist reports, 137
spelling, 82
Steele, Jody, 157
stroke (slash), 79–80
structure in writing, 74–80, 142
Stukeley, William, 13–14
Style Manual: For Authors, Editors and Printers, 80, 173, 179–80

submission checklist, 174
submitted typescript, 173–4
symbolic archaeology, 38, 69
synonym dictionary, 80

table titles, 146
tables, 99, 105, 134–5, 145–6, 173
Taylor, Walter W., 1, 31–2, 64–5
television, 46, 57, 68, 155–6
text references to illustrations and tables, 99–100
textbooks, 37–8, 49–50, 75, 154
Thames and Hudson, 155
Thompson, Edward Herbert, 24–6
three-age system, 62–4
Tilley, Christopher, 69
time taken for publication, 182
trade books, 7, 52–3, 156
Trigger, Bruce, 68
type, bold, 79, 142
italic, 79, 142
types of publication, 9–10, 37, 44, 46–7, 136

University of California, 48
University of Colorado libraries, 151
Uppsala University, 48
using data, 86, 139–40, 153

Wenner-Gren Foundation, 48
Wheeler, Mortimer, 22–3, 29–31, 47, 71, 93, 103
White, J.P., 2
Whitmore, Simon, 6
Willett, Frank, 89
word choice, 76–7, 80–82
processors, 82, 87–8
repetition, 80

writing as a habit, 5
  as a performance, 83
  identifications on illustrations, 101
  methods, 87–8

needs determination, 84–5, 189
plan, 74, 86
work schedule, 84, 163

Yentsch, Anne Elizabeth, 38–9